AN

ASSERTION

OF RIGHT

Tracy C. Coyle

The enormous expense of Governments has provoked
people to think, by making them feel; and when once the
veil begins to rend, it admits not of repair.

Rights of Man, Thomas Paine, 1791

To Mom and Dad, my creators, my endowers, thanks.

To Victoria and CJ, my life and my happiness.

Table of Contents

Preface

"We hold these truths to be self-evident, that all men are created equal, that they are endowed by their Creator with certain unalienable rights, that among these are life, liberty and the pursuit of happiness."[1]

What is a right? Where do rights come from, if they come from anywhere? Are rights a legal fabrication or just acquiescence by others to do what we want established by society or tradition? For Jefferson and many others, the Creator is the only source of rights.

The phrase 'among these' suggests that 'life, liberty and the pursuit of happiness' are just a subset of rights. Are all rights equal or of the same nature? How many rights exist? How many different types of rights exist? The subset offered by Jefferson suggests at least two different types of rights. Life is not aspirational, life either exists or does not and individuals have an infinite set of choices to attempt to pursue or aspire to, happiness.

If God endows individuals with rights, is there a mechanism? Is there a process how and when rights attach or are bestowed? If someone says God brought rain to a drought stricken area, we know the rain came by way of a mechanism we understand scientifically quite well.

The Bible explains how God brought life into an individual:

> *Genesis 2:7 - then the Lord God formed man from the dust of the ground, and breathed into his nostrils the breath of life; and man became a living being.*

In May 2008, during an online debate, I stated the 'endowed by their Creator' origin of rights said nothing of their origin or extent. I stated that we were born with rights, that they were inherent in our existence; which in many ways is no better than 'by their Creator'. I was challenged to state where rights originated, what rights were 'correct' and which were no more than the ranting of a lunatic or the justification of a tyrant. Let me introduce you to my debate antagonist:

> *You are going to have to answer the question of where our rights originate before this discussion can go anywhere. Just saying that we have them isn't an explanation, but the absence of an explanation.*
>
> *The challenge with relying on "rights" as defined by metaphysics is that NOBODY really agrees what those rights are. So to speak in terms of "rights" and demanding your "rights" in a specific context is not really helpful to your argument.*

The challenge galvanized me into spending time and considerably more effort into going beyond 'inherent in our existence' and into giving my positions substance. I established a couple premises. First, the individual is sovereign. We are the masters of ourselves. Our personal actions and needs are our responsibility. We can not transfer that responsibility to others, we can not avoid the consequences of our actions. Even slaves still have absolute control over their own thoughts and physical actions. Nothing can change or allow us to abdicate that status.

Second, all rights are inherent in us. Rights exist because we exist. The foundation of rights can be found in each of us. Each of us has the need to breath, eat, drink, sleep; fulfilling those needs require us to act in specific ways that if interfered with could prevent our continued existence. If we are sovereign, we are responsible first to our selves and our needs.

To honestly take up the challenge, I was going to have to find support for these premises AND where they led me. It took a year to find my starting point. [2]

Introduction

"Ignorance is of a peculiar nature: and once dispelled, it is
impossible to reestablish it. It is not originally a thing of
itself, but is only the absence of knowledge; and though
man may be kept ignorant, he cannot be made ignorant."
Rights of Man, Thomas Paine, 1791

In Thomas Hobbes' (1588-1679) Leviathan (1651), Hobbes
took his observations on the natural state of man...

> "Nature hath made man so equal in the faculties of body and
> mind as that, though there be found one man sometimes
> manifestly stronger in body or of quicker mind that another,
> yet when all is reckoned together the difference between
> man and man is not so considerable..."[3]

...and considered the State necessary for human progress:

> "...that is to say, of getting themselves out from that
> miserable condition of war which is necessarily consequent,
> as has been shown, to the natural passions of men when
> there is no visable power to keep them in awe, and tie them
> by fear of punishment to the performance of their
> covenants..."[4]

Whatever equality of creation Hobbes believed in, he also
believed that man was incorrigible: always at war and always
in need of something to govern him. When John Locke (1632-
1704) struck pen to paper in 1689, he made the same
observation Hobbes declared as a natural state of man:

> "Man being born, as has been proved, with a title to perfect
> freedom and an uncontrolled enjoyment of all the rights and
> privileges of the law of Nature, equally with any other
> man..."[5]

He came to a similar conclusion – government was necessary

"...and that therefore God hath certainly appointed government to restrain the partiality and violence of men. I easily grant that civil government is the proper remedy for the inconveniences of the state of Nature..." [6]

Not just necessary and proper, but with authority forever over all...

"The power that every individual gave the society when he entered into it can never revert to the individuals again, as long as society lasts, but will always remain in the community"[7]

The opening of the New World and the immigration of large numbers of people from the governing institutions of society started to give some evidence that man was not always at war with everyone. Humanity could work together for mutual benefit. Jean-Jacques Rousseau (1712-1778) published The Social Contract in 1762 seeking to:

"...examine whether, in the ordering of society, there can be any reliable and legitimate rule of administration, taking men as they are, and laws as they can be."[8]

After much effort to establish man as the source of legitimate authority for "administration", he all but takes away man's freedom, subjugating it to the Society as controlled by the State, for their freedom and benefit of course.

"In order therefore that the social pact should not be an empty formula, it contains an implicit obligation which alone can give force to the others, that if anyone refuses to obey the general will he will be compelled to do so by the whole body; which means nothing else than that he will be forced to be free; for such is the condition which, giving each citizen to his country, guarantees that he will not depend on any person. This condition is the device that ensures the operation of the political machine."[9]

For our own good has become the reason for all types of tyranny. Edmund Burke (1729-1797), suggested ordered liberty or was it ordered existence?

"I should, therefore, suspend my congratulations on the new liberty of France until I was informed how it had been combined with government, with public force, with the discipline and obedience of armies, with the collection of an effective and well-distributed revenue, with morality and religion, with the solidity of property, with peace and order, with civil and social manners. All these (in their way) are good things, too, and without them liberty is not a benefit whilst it lasts, and is not likely to continue long."[10]

Burke, a favorite of today's conservatives, was firm in his opinions on the French Revolution and the concept of a government by the people:

"It is claimed that "…the people of England have acquired three fundamental rights, all which, with him, compose one system, and lie together in one short sentence; namely, that we have acquired a right
    "To choose our own governors."
    "To cashier them for misconduct."
    "To frame a government for ourselves."
"This new, and hitherto unheard-of, bill of rights, though made in the name of the whole people, belongs to those gentlemen and their faction only. The body of the people of England have no share in it. They utterly disclaim it. They will resist the practical assertion of it with their lives and fortunes. They are bound to do so by the laws of their country, made at the time of that very Revolution which is appealed to in favour of the fictitious rights claimed by the Society which abuses its name."[11]

And:

> "The very idea of the fabrication of a new government is enough to fill us with disgust and horror."[12]

Thomas Paine (1737-1809) writing in Rights of Man (1791) destroyed Burke's assertions on the benefits and necessity of rule by monarchies:

> "A greater absurdity cannot present itself to the understanding of man than what Mr. Burke offers to his readers. He tells them, and he tells the world to come, that a certain body of men who existed a hundred years ago, made a law, and that there does not now exist in the Nation, nor ever will, nor ever can, a power to alter it. Under how many subtilties or absurdities has the divine right to govern been imposed on the credulity of mankind! Mr. Burke has discovered a new one, and he has shortened his journey to Rome by appealing to the power of this infallible Parliament of former days; and he produces what it has done as of divine authority, for that power must certainly be more than human which no human power to the end of time can alter."[13]

Paine's passionate arguments in Common Sense helped to fan the flame of independence. Paine thought government necessary, but the best government was the simplest:

> "Society in every state is a blessing, but government even in its best state is but a necessary evil, in its worse state an intolerable one."[14]

> "Here then is the origin and rise of government; namely, a mode rendered necessary by the inability of moral virtue to govern the world; here too is the design and end of government, viz. Freedom and security."[15]

Thomas Jefferson (1743-1826) of course disagreed with Burke. In the Declaration of Independence (1776) he took square aim at government and fired a devastating broadside:

> "Governments are instituted among Men, deriving their just powers from the consent of the governed, That whenever any Form of Government becomes destructive of these ends, it is the Right of the People to alter or to abolish it, and to institute new Government, laying its foundation on such principles and organizing its powers in such form, as to them shall seem most likely to effect their Safety and Happiness."

Government was and is the servant; the people, as sovereigns, were the masters and only the free exercise of sovereignty by the people gave government any legitimacy and authority. Fundamental rights and authority began and remained with the individual. Government and society were beneficial as long as they served the individual.

It is a natural progression from individual to family to community to society but at no point is government as an entity either natural or preordained despite the claim of Hobbes. In the far past, man was a beast and needed to be tamed. The American Revolution said no longer. Man could order his affairs. Individuals had the right to do so. Government was but a tool of society, not the pinnacle of it:

> "Some writers have so confounded society with government, as to leave little or no distinction between them;"[16]

Paine was wrong about one thing: society was not and is not in every state a blessing, as John Stuart Mill (1806-1873) would note in On Liberty (1859):

"Society can and does execute its own mandates: and if it issues wrong mandates instead of right, or any mandates at all in things with which it ought not to meddle, it practises a social tyranny more formidable than many kinds of political oppression, since, though not usually upheld by such extreme penalties, it leaves fewer means of escape, penetrating much more deeply into the details of life, and enslaving the soul itself. Protection, therefore, against the tyranny of the magistrate is not enough; there needs protection also against the tyranny of the prevailing opinion and feeling; against the tendency of society to impose, by other means than civil penalties, its own ideas and practices as rules of conduct on those who dissent from them; to fetter the development, and, if possible, prevent the formation, of any individuality not in harmony with its ways, and compel all characters to fashion themselves upon the model of its own."

His response made clear the limits of a beneficial society (or State):

"…to assert one very simple principle, as entitled to govern absolutely the dealings of society with the individual in the way of compulsion and control, whether the means used be physical force in the form of legal penalties, or the moral coercion of public opinion. That principle is, that the sole end for which mankind are warranted, individually or collectively in interfering with the liberty of action of any of their number, is self-protection. That the only purpose for which power can be rightfully exercised over any member of a civilized community, against his will, is to prevent harm to others."

Looking back at the writings of Hobbes, Locke, Paine, Jefferson and Mill, the thread is there to follow: man (beast that he could be) was the source of legitimate government and authorities. But history is full of examples where once some men were given the power to constrain others that they exemplified the worst base passions they were empowered to prevent. If a system of constraints could be formulated that would limit mans more base passions, without creating despots and tyrannies, the result would benefit all. Jefferson laid the foundation in the Declaration of Independence:

"That to secure these rights, governments are instituted among men, deriving their just powers from the consent of the governed. That whenever any form of government becomes destructive to these ends, it is the right of the people to alter or to abolish it, and to institute new government, laying its foundation on such principles and organizing its powers in such form, as to them shall seem most likely to effect their safety and happiness."

Asking where rights come from suggests the notion that there is an institution, document or Creator standing by to anoint each child at birth with a package and stamp proclaiming 'rights holder'. Unless I missed something or my parents are holding back, I don't recall ever seeing such a package or stamp. It is clear that Jefferson believed rights were an inherent part of our existence.

Is there some point or process whereby their existence becomes inherent, some mechanism we can determine, rather than rely on a statement on a historical document that is certainly the product of our less knowledgeable past?

The world and society were slowly evolving 230 years ago, a process that has sped up considerably in the last 50 years. It is time to revisit the questions and some of the observations. In his introduction to Common Sense, Thomas Paine offered more hope for his point of view than I do mine:

"Perhaps the sentiments contained in the following pages are not yet sufficiently fashionable to procure them general favor; a long habit of not thinking a thing wrong, gives it a superficial appearance of being right, and raises at first a formidable outcry in defence of custom. But the tumult soon subsides. Time makes more converts than reason."

In Part One, my goal is to offer a definition of rights, state an explicit origin and establish their limitations. In Part Two, I look at how rights serve as a foundation for government's management of rights and in Part Three I discuss some of the issues and considerations.

Part One: The Origin of Rights

...we must consider what state all men are naturally in...[17]

The natural state of We, the people...

Alive. We know the mechanism now. One sperm, leaving the man, one egg leaving the ovary. Both alive. And when the sperm finds the egg, cleaving the surface and entering, becoming one. Alive.

The zygote and the gamete are both living human cells. Carrying genetic material, by themselves they are dead ends. Only joined together do we get true potential. One cell carries the genetic blueprint of a human life but without purpose, without a goal; it can do nothing except what is already written in the blueprint.

The genetic blueprint begins a very basic cellular function: Grow, divide, grow, divide. The cell becomes millions of cells but there are no decisions being made, no choices are being considered. Eventually the cells begin to differentiate, to specialize and still there is no free will, no decisions; no choices are being made.

Yes, the single cell and all the additional cells are living human cells. They have no liberty, no free will to pursue anything. There is no independent life except what is provided it to them. There must be another step taken before their potential can be realized.

As the cells differentiate, structures form and coordination between the various parts form patterns we recognize as a 'human'. The coordination is not choice; it is not a consciousness imposing direction or control. The child, however recognizable, lacks the structure and internal integrity to exercise any control over itself. S/he is still just following the genetic blueprint already provided.

15

Yet, somewhere down the line, after 18-20 weeks, the child stirs.

"Life is the immediate gift of God, a right inherent by nature in every individual; and it begins in contemplation of law as soon as an infant is able to stir in the mother's womb." [18]

The first actions are not according to any blueprint, they are not written into the genes. No protein map that says on the 149th day, kick the left leg. Is it a choice? A decision made? Or just a random firing of neurons beginning to establish pathways and connections?

We know the brain begins to show activity well before this point, but all the action appears to be 'internal' to the brain structure.

"First, intermittent electro-encephalographic bursts in both cerebral hemispheres are first seen at 20 weeks gestation; they become sustained at 22 weeks and bilaterally synchronous at 26 to 27 weeks." [19]

Despite the growing complexity of brain activity, there does not appear to be a 'thought process'[20] going on. The child's brain is reacting to its body, which is reacting to the environment it is in. Stimulus causes reaction. The mother hums a tune, eats a spicy meal, becomes scared, or becomes excited. Each of these events causes the environment the child is in to change and the child's body reacts. Specific sounds excite or calm the child. Is the child thinking, "ah, mom is singing that song I like"? Or does the mother's state of mind while singing cause a release of hormones that cause a specific reaction in the brain of the child? Is this thinking? Is this the infant brain making choices? Relax? Rest? We don't know. Our technology can register the reaction, see the change. We can measure the change in hormones, know that they have an impact, but if actual physical control of the body by a specific 'thought' is occurring, it does not appear to be anything more

16

than a localized biological response to some stimuli. It does not appear that the brain is telling a part of the body, move.

Those first thoughts, maybe fleeting sparks of awareness, belong uniquely, within the brain. For the entire life of the child each thought will occur away from anyone else's knowledge or understanding - unless s/he chooses to share them with others. And from those first thoughts, the plan built into our genes begins to turn over control of the body to the consciousness growing and learning within.

"There be in animals two sorts of motions peculiar to them: One called vital, begun in generation, and continued without interruption through their whole life; such as the course of blood, the pulse, the breathing, the concoction, nutrition, excretion, etc; to which motion there needs no help of imagination; the other is animal motion, otherwise voluntary motion; as to go, to speak, to move any of our limbs, in such manner as is first fancied in our minds.

...And because going, speaking, and the like voluntary motions depend always upon a precedent thought of whither, which way, and what, it is evident that the imagination is the first internal beginning of all voluntary motion."[21]

Many of the first actions we take as humans are based on direct reaction to specific internal stimulus. The actions are basic, almost completely automatic. Our bodies make demands, we respond. From our birth until our death, we will seek food when hungry, we will seek sleep when tired and we will seek a bathroom (or similar) when we need to relieve ourselves. The process of learning how to react, how to respond to stimulus, how to control our bodies begins as the brain begins to assume control over the body before birth and continues with certain immediacy afterwards.

With very few exceptions, this is the process every human goes through. Whether our parents were rich or poor, educated or not, king or pauper, each of us began this way. We are all born with certain characteristics regardless of race, gender, class, religion or income. We all have a heart that beats, lungs that breathe, a body that moves and a brain that thinks. This is the equality of creation, the human condition.

"Nature hath made man so equal in the faculties of body and mind as that, though there be found one man sometimes manifestly stronger in body or of quicker mind that another, yet when all is reckoned together the difference between man and man is not so considerable as that one man can thereupon claim to himself any benefit to which another may not pretend as well as he."[22]

"But man, besides the marvelous disposition of his body, has likewise a rational soul, which eminently discriminates him from brutes. It is by this noble part of himself that he thinks, and is capable of forming just ideas of the different objects, that occur to him; of comparing them together; of inferring from known principles unknown truths; of passing a solid judgment on the mutual fitness or agreement of things, as well as on the relations they bear to us; of deliberating on what is proper or improper to be done; and of determining consequently to act one way or other. The mind recollects what is past, joins it with the present, and extends its views to futurity. It is capable of penetrating into the causes, progress, and consequences of things, and of discovering, as it were at one glance, the intire course of life, which enables it to lay in a store of such things, as are necessary for making a happy career. Besides, in all this, it is not subject to a constant series of uniform and invariable operations, but finds itself at liberty to act or not to act, to suspend its actions and motions, to direct and manage them as it thinks proper."[23]

The Law of Nature or the Character of Nature

What is the law of nature?

"I answer that, Law is a rule and measure of acts, whereby man is induced to act or is restrained from acting: for "lex" [law] is derived from "ligare" [to bind], because it binds one to act. Now the rule and measure of human acts is the reason, which is the first principle of human acts, as is evident from what has been stated above (Q1:1, ad 3); since it belongs to the reason to direct to the end, which is the first principle in all matters of action, according to the Philosopher."[24]

Thomas Aquinas (1225-1274) in Summa Theologica (1265-1274) states that law is a rule and measure of acts that man must take or be restricted from taking. The acts in question are those necessary to human happiness.

"Consequently the law must needs regard principally the relationship to happiness"[25]

Aquinas spends time on the nature of law and reaches the conclusion that natural law is based on and supports the needs of individual.

"Consequently the first principle of practical reason is one founded on the notion of good, viz. that "good is that which all things seek after." Hence this is the first precept of law, that "good is to be done and pursued, and evil is to be avoided." All other precepts of the natural law are based upon this: so that whatever the practical reason naturally apprehends as man's good (or evil) belongs to the precepts of the natural law as something to be done or avoided.

Since, however, good has the nature of an end, and evil, the nature of a contrary, hence it is that all those things to which man has a natural inclination, are naturally apprehended by reason as being good, and consequently as objects of pursuit, and their contraries as evil, and objects of avoidance. Wherefore according to the order of natural inclinations, is the order of the precepts of the natural law. Because in man there is first of all an inclination to good in accordance with the nature which he has in common with all substances: inasmuch as every substance seeks the preservation of its own being, according to its nature: and by reason of this inclination, whatever is a means of preserving human life, and of warding off its obstacles, belongs to the natural law. Secondly, there is in man an inclination to things that pertain to him more specially, according to that nature which he has in common with other animals: and in virtue of this inclination, those things are said to belong to the natural law, "which nature has taught to all animals", such as sexual intercourse, education of offspring and so forth."[26]

Hobbes and Locke suggest that natural law is a rule determined by reason – and therefore accessible to all capable of reason – which applies to everyone, that we are all equal and no one should harm another.

"A law of nature, lex naturalis, is a precept, or general rule, found out by reason, by which a man is forbidden to do that which is destructive of his life, or taketh away the means of preserving the same, and to omit that by which he thinketh it may be best preserved."[27]

"The state of Nature has a law of Nature to govern it, which obliges every one, and reason, which is that law, teaches all mankind who will but consult it, that being all equal and independent, no one ought to harm another in his life, health, liberty or possessions;"[28]

"When in the Course of human events it becomes necessary for one people to dissolve the political bands which have connected them with another and to assume among the powers of the earth, the separate and equal station to which the Laws of Nature and of Nature's God entitle them, a decent respect to the opinions of mankind requires that they should declare the causes which impel them to the separation."

Hobbes and Locke (and by implication, Jefferson) suggest that the law of nature has two components: state – that condition of being equal and independent, and consequence - the result of reason no one can harm another.

In all of these writings, each writer notes that we are part of nature but with the ability to reason and that sets us apart from the animals. I don't disagree, but if reason sets us apart, it does not remove us from a state of nature.

Of the state of nature

Nature has no reason, it does however have purpose. We know that in each species, there is a set of characteristics that apply to all offspring. We know there is a considerable range of possibilities within those characteristics: weight, height, potential for intelligence, propensity for exceeding – for better or worse – the parents. As Hobbes noted, despite the range of possibilities, there is not a significant difference between humans [29]

These natural variations give rise to diversity in the population. It is the purpose of nature to encourage this diversity. However, nature does not need that all individuals survive or that any one should prevail. The goal of nature is to give each species the chance to grow and thrive, but it is indifferent to individual life. To Nature each individual is as good for it's purpose as any other.

Each species however has a great desire that each individual survive. Unlike Natures indifference, each species seeks to nurture those individuals most likely to help carry the species into the future. For the weak, infirm, and elderly incapable of perpetuation of the species, there is no future. Species seek the strongest at the expense of the weakest and will cull the non-performers. Each species has a biological imperative that force beneficial (to the species) behaviors on individuals. In humans we call it morality.[30]

For nature, moral behavior perpetuates diversity and promotes healthy competition between species. Moral behavior that perpetuates the species is 'right' and behavior that fails to support the future is 'wrong'.

Nature may be indifferent to the individual, but we are not. Unlike other 'species', we have free will. We can ignore the imperatives and support the weak, the infirm and the elderly. We have the ability and liberty to choose for ourselves; individuals can choose to ignore or conform to the purpose of nature.

> "And because the condition of man (as hath been declared in the precedent chapter) is a condition of war of every one against everyone, in which case everyone is governed by his own reason…"[31]

The Story of Billy

I need to take some time to explain a couple of words, define them if you wish. In order to do so I have to tell a story, it has elements of truth, but did not actually happen. Try to remember that later.

I was first born. My parents, having been born and raised on an island, spent much of their youth swimming in the ocean. Their children were going to get the opportunity to swim too. Although not as big as the ocean, Lake Michigan was big enough to serve their purpose. My brother Steve was born ten months later. A third child, Billy, came 21 months further along. My sister Ann, brother Eddie and sister Elizabeth followed in similar intervals.

We grew up with above ground pools in the yard every summer and we spent camping vacations as much in the water as on it fishing. Learning to swim was less a chore than a necessity! When I was five my father took me out on a boat a mile offshore and threw me overboard. "Swim to shore" he yelled as he rowed back. And I did. The next summer, it was Steve's turn. Finally, two years later, Billy got the same, equal treatment. And he drowned (remember, story....)

"…that all men are created equal…"

But we are not equal. We have different situations, abilities and skills that make certain tasks easier for some, more difficult for others. There are other aspects or characteristics that might be the focus of that part of the Declaration, but physical equality is not it.

We often talk about how we all want to be treated equally. Here, three kids were all treated equally. Except I left out an important fact: Billy had muscular dystrophy. He COULD swim, but the distance was just beyond his ability. Had my father been fair? Three children, all exposed to swimming from an early age, all good swimmers, all given the same task. We all had been treated equally. Yet, my father did not take my brother's condition into consideration. Should he have?

In truth, very often we do NOT want to be treated equally[32]. We want all the factors to be taken into consideration; we want to be treated fairly, we want justice.

Had my father treated Billy differently, he might have survived the swim, but by lowering expectations, his accomplishment would have not been the same as mine or Steve. The assumption that Billy could not accomplish the task and therefore had to be given a different benchmark is the prejudice of low expectations. In tens of thousands of situations every day, we as a society are guilty of this prejudice, this fairness. Every time we lower expectations, lower the benchmarks for society, we make the next generation less likely to match or exceed us.

Is our choice equality or fairness? I don't think so. But it is clear that they have been inappropriately applied. Fairness seems so…fair. What could be wrong about wanting to be fair, about wanting justice?

23

The one place where justice and fairness have become the prevailing impulse is in our courts. For those that want to point out that equality under the law is the ideal I will note that after spending ten years watching our courts (federal and local), equality is the last thing expected or provided. When people are in court, they demand that the courts be fair, they want the court to take the entirety of circumstances into consideration, not just the law. Our courts are no longer courts of law but courts of justice and equity. Equity and justice in the courts is institutionalized inequality. Justice is unequal because we are fundamentally, unequal. To have a claim between two unequal parties resolved to the satisfaction of both parties is to have an unequal outcome.

Why is the desire to treat everyone fairly wrong? It is about not giving everyone the same benchmark. It creates different classes of people. It creates divisions; it suggests that some people are born to lead and others are born to serve.

For the rest of my story about Billy, Dad really didn't just leave him out there. He stayed close and let Billy have a few breathers that Steve and I didn't get. But he still had to swim the mile and he did – we wouldn't have let him get away with anything less. There were the same expectations, and the same demands made on Billy as the rest of us kids. He was given an assist at the appropriate points but was not relieved of his responsibilities. He did not, ever, ask to be treated differently. He was expected to swim the mile and nothing less than that goal was acceptable. But he was given additional assistance in keeping with his abilities. It is respect that demands both, equal benchmarks and fair treatment.

Respect is not making the finish line different for people, but in acknowledging the differences in everyone's abilities. Par on a golf course does not change because the player is not a professional. Handicapping systems address different skill levels.

It is the hardest thing for us as humans to do: treat each other with respect. Requiring Billy to swim the same distance was treating him with respect. It was not saying —you can't, so don't bother. Institutionally, we created affirmative action to treat others differently based not on their own circumstances, but on systemic circumstances. It changed the finish lines, changed par for the course and the result was not respect, but belief that minorities couldn't make it to the finish line at all.

I am not sure why people are so disrespectful in this way; out of a sense of guilt, or pity? It is extremely damaging to those being disrespected and when it is applied to groups, dangerous to them and us.

Of the consequence of nature

Hobbes and Locke may reason that as a consequence of all being equal and independent, we should not harm ourselves or each other, but that ignores the nature that they find us in, 'a state of war'. Here is how I think they get to their conclusion and why it is wrong:

> "When, in the course of human events, it becomes necessary for one people to dissolve the political bands which have connected them with another, and to assume among the powers of the earth, the separate and equal station to which the laws of nature and of nature's God entitle them..."

All equal does not mean that each is the same as others, all equal means none have more claim or authority than any other on resources needed for survival. As the species grows in number, competition for resources increases. The diversity inherent in human characteristics grants a natural INEQUALITY in abilities; some individuals will be able to take more than their share of resources. It benefits some individuals (especially the weakest) to work together to insure everyone has access to resources and that none exceed their share of those resources[33]. In general, such a result will be less than optimum from Nature's point of view.

Hobbes and Locke are religious men. They count all humanity as part of creation, created in God's image. For them to leave the weak or infirm defenseless violates every principle they believe are part of the very foundation of our existence. It is not objective reason or a law of nature that all should survive and be protected, it is a Commandment from God. Nature is God's creation and all of Creation is under His care. Hobbes and Locke could reach no other reasoned conclusion.

Nature has no such reason. Nature does not need nor expect that all individuals survive or procreate. Competition within and between species is one of the characteristics of the law of nature - survival of the fittest.[34] Once an individual ceases being useful, a species is as indifferent as nature itself.[35]

Free will gives humans the opportunity to make different choices than the law of nature would dictate. We are part of Nature, but we can not walk away from the weak, the infirm, and the no longer useful aged. We are faced with a knowledge of mortality and specifically our own and that drives different choices.

In early humans, competition for resources often resulted in death. The only change that has occurred over the centuries is we have channeled that competition into non-fatal (usually) sports. Species (even homosapiens) continue to encourage competition; the biological imperative is strong.

Unlike nature, humans can impose reason over competition; we can impose free will over the biological imperative. Liberty is not bound by nature. The law of nature is for the unthinking animals. Humanity, expressing a thought, exceeds the limits of nature and sets for itself, each one of us, our own path through life.

Such is the human condition: a part of nature, but by free will, unbound from the indifference of nature and free to choose compassion over competition.

I think....

Thought is the physical action of the brain. For a thought to occur the brain must have structure and integrity, it must have resources such as nutrients and energy, and it must have impulse such as internal or external stimulus.

Never[36], have our thoughts been subject to review, interpretation, interception or modification by another person. A thought is the sole property of the individual. We may choose to share them with others, we may act in ways that people can interpret as a response to a thought we have had, but the thought is ours alone forever. The owner of the thought is without question, the human in which it is formed; it can not be taken by another, it can not be restricted, or limited by another.

Thought is an expression of free will. It requires effort on the part of the individual. Whether the thought continues, whether it is expanded, restricted or discarded is the choice and responsibility of the individual.

This is freedom – the source of liberty. The absolute, unrestricted act of thought that finds its expression in every single human being. It does not find its source in government or society; by document or decree. It occurs without leave or permission from any or all. It is inherent in every human, by nature of our existence. It can not be denied or refused; it is inalienable. The absolute freedom exists as long as we exist.

If we own the thought and the action that expresses that thought then we own the consequences of those actions. You can not separate the act from its consequences any more than the action from the thought. This ownership is the essence of individuality.

> "In the part which merely concerns himself, his independence is, of right, absolute. Over himself, over his own body and mind, the individual is sovereign".[37]

In order to satisfy the needs of the human condition, we need to express our thoughts with certain actions. All actions necessary for the continuation of an individual are fundamental to their existence and the need to freely express those acts is absolute.

"But though this be a state of liberty, yet it is not a state of licence; though man in that state have an uncontrollable liberty to dispose of his person or possessions, yet he has not liberty to destroy himself or so much as any creature in his possession, but where some nobler use than its bare preservation calls for it."[38]

The actions are required because we exist and because our existence depends on them.[39] Before there is an act, there must be a will to act. And before there is a will to act, there must be a thought. Without thought, there is no free will. It can not be restricted except by our own desire/choice. It can not be denied except by our own limitations.

Two impulses create thought: needs and desire. We share needs – they are part of the human condition. Every human needs air to breathe, food to nourish and water to drink. These needs are among the primary or fundamental internal impulses that stimulate thought. Desire is that aspect that Jefferson called the 'pursuit of happiness'; it is no less fundamental to the human condition. We are more than bare existence; we seek more than just breathing, eating and existing. We seek companionship and we seek to extend ourselves with children and accomplishments. The actions that allow us these pursuits are as necessary to our well being as the food we eat. Each of these needs stimulate thoughts that seek to be expressed by actions.

Thought exists within the individual, unless the individual expresses that thought, either directly or by expressing an action, it remains out of sight from others.[40] I choose when to express a thought – it is my responsibility to consider the consequences. This is the foundation of privacy. Privacy is ownership of thought and the individual ability to limit the expression of that thought.

...therefore, fundamentally, I do...

What actions are fundamental? If eating is fundamental is gathering food fundamental? Is preparing or cultivating food fundamental? Any action necessary for the free expression of a fundamental act is not subject to limit, restriction or denial EXCEPT when the act threatens others.

The individual has the need to express fundamental thoughts and to defend against attempts to limit, restrict or deny those needs. Actions by individuals, groups or societies to limit, restrict or deny that freedom are a threat to the individual and all individuals and are therefore subject to any action to prevent or eliminate that threat.

Personal responsibility

The structure that allows thought, the thought held and expressed by an act and the consequences of that act form an unbroken physical chain unique to each individual. This is the foundation of personal responsibility.

Responsibility to ourselves: We have the need to fulfill fundamental needs and we assert our freedom to do so.

Responsibility to others: We are responsible to ensure that the consequences of our acts do not harm or interfere in the liberties of others.

Any stimulus can provoke a thought, but our free will determines what happens next. Do we keep the thought or dismiss it? Do we express the thought through action? These are our choices; this is our free will in action. We can be coerced, threatened or encouraged but it is our choice what happens next. It is the fundamental nature of thought that gives us both the ownership and the responsibility for them. Many people will make lots of arguments that coercion can be extreme, that stimulus can be so well known and defined that specific thoughts can be forced to be expressed. In each and every case, once the thought exists, it is the free will of the individual, the choice of the individual, to dismiss, hold or express a thought. Individuals are solely and always responsible for the expression of a thought by their actions and the consequences thereof. I can not hold you responsible for my thoughts and actions. I own my thoughts, I choose to express them by acting. I am responsible for them. You can not hold me responsible for your thoughts and actions. You own your thoughts, you choose to express them. You are responsible for them. Each of us has thoughts, expresses them and is responsible for those actions. As long as those actions do not threaten another, there is no limit to the number of possible actions we may take.

> "…though man in that state have an uncontrollable liberty to dispose of his person or possessions, yet he has not liberty to destroy himself…"[41]

In this Locke was wrong. He said it but either couldn't see it or wouldn't see it. Slavery was/is a choice. If every thought belongs to you and every act and consequence likewise, then being a slave is a consequence of the choice to accept servitude or the alternative (often death). There is no slavery except by choice:

> "For whenever he finds the hardship of his slavery outweigh the value of his life, it is in his power, by resisting the will of his master, to draw down on himself the death he desires."[42]

Death can be a choice. When the burdens of life exceed the value an individual holds for it, they choose to die or not to continue to fight for life. For many, this is the final expression of a fundamental thought and they have just as much freedom to express it as any other fundamental act.

We can not give someone else the responsibility to express our fundamental thoughts and actions any more than we can give someone the responsibility for the consequences of our acts. We own the need to express thoughts, the need to protect our ability to do so and the consequences from having done so.

We do not have the freedom to act because others have give us that freedom, but because we assert the need to act and must do so regardless or in spite of any act or belief of others.

Attempts to restrict the free expression of fundamental actions are a threat to the individual. It is a fundamental characteristic of the human condition to desire to continue to exist. The species seeks to maximize the individual and each individual seeks no less. Threats to the individual can be dealt with by any means such that the threat ceases to be either imminent or persistent.

"And consequently it is a precept, or general rule of reason: that everyman ought to endeavor to peace, as far as he hope of obtaining it; and when he cannot obtain it, that he may seek and use all helps and advantages of war. The first branch of which rule containeth the first and fundamental law of nature, which is to seek peace and follow it. The second, the sum of the right of nature, which is: by all means we can defend ourselves."[43]

"In transgressing the law of Nature* the offender declares himself to live by another rule than that of reason and common equity, which is that measure God has set to the actions of men for their mutual security, and so he becomes dangerous to mankind;
....the execution of the law of nature is in that state put into every man's hands, whereby everyone has a right to punish the transgressors of that law to such a degree as may hinder its violation."[44]

31

* that being all equal and independent, no one ought harm another in his life, health, liberty or possessions.

Obviously Locke is not suggesting that the character of "equal and independent' is being transgressed, but rather the violation of consequence or the precept that one should not harm another or self. It is the state of nature that competition exists and that competition is often fatal. Competition does not always exist between individuals and species. If the needs of the individual or group are being met, there is no competition for resources. Among humans, if each individual's needs are being met, competition is a form of social interaction.[45] Unlike species of animals, humans have the ability to work together (in situations of scarce resources) rather than in competition. Once again, humans can exceed nature by exercising free will. However, individuals (or groups) that act to obtain more than their needs at the expense of others have interfered in the ability of others to satisfy their needs, such an act is the nature of the transgression.

There is nothing in the human condition that prevents such transgressions except free will. These types of acts are threats to others. When they are acts expressed solely for the pleasure of individuals, we call them evil. When these evil/threatening thoughts are expressed, it is part of the human condition to seek to limit, restrict or stop them. This is the foundation of self-defense.

I have the need to breathe, if you attempt to prevent me from fulfilling that need, you have proclaimed to all humanity that you are willing to deprive others of their needs; that your reasoning has determined denying the needs of another is acceptable or desirable. Such reasoning is a threat that needs to be faced or addressed, as you would do any such threat to your existence.

The Island

Last night you went to bed, comfortable in your life. This
morning you awoke, alone, on an island somewhere in the
middle of an unknown sea or ocean. After the required yelling
to find out who is playing a trick on you, or where the cameras
are hiding, you determine you are, in fact, alone. Your sense of
organization kicks in, or is it just your hunger, and you set off
to find the necessary requirements for sustaining your life, at
least for the next couple of hours.

A day spent exploring your island confirms a growing
suspicion that if you are going to survive, it will be up to your
imagination, your abilities and the resources available to you.
Today, you are the king of your domain. Survivability is the
only rule. Over the next several weeks, you gather food, water
and the materials to build some shelter. You took what was
needed, you choose a place to build, and you soiled the
previously pristine environment. You did what was necessary
to survive. Soon, certain routines became established, but
whether something was done on a Monday or a Thursday was
as irrelevant as whether it was Monday or Thursday. You
sought food and water when necessary, repaired your shelter
when it needed it. Whether you sat back and waited for
whatever came next or strove to alter your circumstances, each
day was devoted to ensuring the next.

Without exception, every action you took was either to further
your survival, or increase the comfort of your situation. You
required no permission, no license or grant. If you could
imagine an action, if you had the ability and the resources, you
could take that action. Every action had direct consequences. A
failure to obtain water meant thirst. Cause and effect came
unbuffered. Soon you learned which actions would benefit you,
and which would make you uncomfortable or take you to the
brink of death. Those choices became rules for your survival. It
doesn't take many false steps to realize the need to consider
both choice and outcome. Yet, there is nothing denying the
freedom to express whatever thought comes to your mind.

No one granted you that freedom. It was not handed to you, or provided by decree. That ability to act with complete freedom is inherent in the situation. Alone on an island, there is no government or society to grant liberties or impose limits on your actions. On the island, you have the complete freedom to act in any way that your imagination, your abilities, the resources and the consequences allow. You are the king of the realm, the sovereign of the island.

Then one day, another person appeared. After the requisite yelling and shouting, you stood staring at each other. Effective immediately, all your resources were cut in half...or were they? What did you owe this new person? You had already ascertained food and water resources, built shelter and established your domain. What claim did this new person have to what you had worked so hard to establish?

Here was someone, like you, stranded. A short conversation revealed he too went to sleep one night and woke up to find himself relocated, no lock, no stock, no barrel. Although two would now divide your available resources, you gained the additional human resource of new imagination, new abilities and a second pair of hands. Knowing that your food and water resources would be sufficient to support both of you, you offered your new domain partner support and friendship. You would teach your friend the rules you learned the hard way and in return, he offered friendship and a chance to double your labor pool.

As of that day, your freedom to express yourself completely and freely ended. Your ability to express yourself did not end with the appearance of a second person, you imposed a limit on it. Society, such that it exists on the island, imposes limitations upon you. It is done with your agreement because you want to 'improve' your situation on the island, not create dissension. This is the fundamental purpose of society, to create a means for individuals to freely express their actions and to establish boundaries for each member in doing so. For the benefit of all, each of us gives up some freedom to act. Our ability to express ourselves does not disappear, we voluntarily limit the options we are willing to exercise.

Limits on the free expression of thought

How many of the actions we take for granted today didn't exist three thousand years ago? How many actions are based on knowledge that didn't exist two hundred years ago? Today, children are taught actions in elementary school based on knowledge that was unique to specialists just a decade or two ago. As knowledge grows[46] humans take that information and combine it in new and unique ways, thinking new thoughts that need new actions to express them. While the number of possible acts is infinite, there are only three types of limits on the ability to express thoughts through actions:

Limits by Nature: Knowledge, ability and resources.
Limits by Self: Consequences, free will.
Limits by Force: Individual, State/government.

Limits By Nature

There are natural limits on the actions that individuals express. As many will attest to, I am tone deaf. I can sing, but most people want me to avoid it at all costs. When I sing it generally offends people in earshot. The first person to sing did not know about scales or tone. They just 'sang'. (I acknowledge the first 'singing' was probably more like humming, non-information bearing sounds that were pleasing to the singer and hopeful those around him or her.)

There is a foundation of knowledge that must exist prior to the thoughts that require a new action; Individuals are limited by their own knowledge and abilities and any thought they express is equally limited. Each new action is based on the knowledge and actions of those that preceded it.

The ability and knowledge to act are part of the human condition. Without the ability to make sounds, there is no

35

singing. Without the ability to hear, there is no need (or desire) for singing. A person without vocal cords can not sing; this does not mean that they are denied the freedom to sing. The lack of vocal cords limits their ability to act. Singing exists in the knowledge base of humanity and is therefore available to all with the ability to express it.

The knowledge base of actions belongs to all humans. Once established, the action is universal even to those of us without the ability. If one person lacks the resources or ability to act specifically, the act still exists but not for that person.

Some actions are so basic that only individual abilities, knowledge and resources will limit their expression. With few exceptions, every individual will be able to express them as their abilities as humans expand with their knowledge. The range of actions has expanded slowly as history progressed. Limited access to natural resources and individual abilities made basic actions all that could be imagined. Small groups of nomadic humans formed to expand the abilities and resources available so that they could express their few actions with fewer inherent limitations. A new action might be expressed in China but not seen in Europe for decades or even centuries. Other actions were resource dependent to the extent that groups closely guarded access to the resource, limiting the ability of other groups to know or express an action such as bronze making. Every new resource would prompt a flurry of innovation of thought and action.

Every action requires physical qualities and knowledge that the action is possible. For most basic actions, the physical qualities necessary exist in virtually all of us, but the knowledge must be learned. From sitting up, to walking, to eating, to sex, humans spend years learning to use the physical qualities of the human body. Many of the basic actions humans take are fundamental – they satisfy a basic need of the human body. They are also often beneficial – they have a range of possible actions that can equally satisfy the basic need.

For those that lack an ability (deafness for example), some

individuals will be able to overcome the obstacles or limitations. Others will learn new abilities, or obtain resources not previously available. But not everyone will be able express every action. It does not make the actions less universal.

Our ancestors could not imagine knives or forks because they had no knowledge of metallurgy or even (far enough back) tool making. The knowledge base was shallow, the abilities available to them limited. For them, all acts were fundamental. The need to provide food and shelter left little time for anything else.

We truly stand on the shoulders of our ancestors. Our knowledge base, our universe of actions has been established by the painstaking acts, thoughts and imaginations of millions of forebearers. Every act had consequences and only through trial and error, success or death, accomplishment or failure did humanity learn which acts were beneficial. Humans spend their waking time in thought and action. The process of learning determines which thoughts deserve action and what acts deserve repetition. As the consequences of acts are learned, new knowledge is combined with the existing and new thoughts occur. The process is repeated in each of us throughout our lives, it is part of the human condition, a consequence of our characteristics. It can no more be restricted or denied than breathing.

Beneficial actions ensure, assist, improve or satisfy the needs of the human condition. I asked earlier if eating is a fundamental act, what would procuring or preparing food be? Such actions are the nature of beneficial acts. The range of actions that are possible in order accomplish beneficial tasks are broader than fundamental actions. Breathing is breathing; not many options to accomplish it. Eating is fundamental, but what is eaten, when, how, how much are all variables with various degrees of freedom. Beneficial actions are still necessary actions and have the same demand on freedom of expression, but we can control the expression of such acts well enough to consider the consequences. Beneficial acts are the expression of liberty and the pursuit of happiness. They are necessary for the health and well being of humans and therefore are part of the human condition.

I knew a woman many years ago that gave birth to a child with no swallow reflex. The fundamental act of eating was unavailable to the child. It was painful to watch her deal with the slow death of her child. Many of us take eating for granted. It is one of those 'bodily' functions that we just do. But any parent will tell you that babies and eating are a messy combination. Our physical ability to eat is built in, but we must still be taught to eat. From a basic eating process to the more creative preparation and savoring of a seven course meal, we learn TO eat, WHAT to eat and even when to eat. Satisfying a fundamental need can often be done using beneficial acts.

Learning what foods are safe or useful has been a human endeavor from the beginning of our time. A child is exposed to many foods that have already been vetted by his/her parents. How often have we wondered how and why someone decided something would be good to eat? The entire concept of caviar makes my stomach lurch yet many people love the texture and taste. (YUK!) Over thousands of years humans have built up a knowledge base of acceptable foods that include a significant portion of the plant and animal matter on the planet. Yet, even acceptable foods to a parent sometimes are bad for the child. The learning process must be repeated for each human. Our learning process did not just include which foods were acceptable, but how they were prepared. Consider wheat. Tools to plant, harvest, mill, and cook all had to be developed and tested. We mill the grain, combine it with water and other items. Each act had to be expressed, the consequences determined and the results assessed. If the act was beneficial, it could be used again and it could lead to further developments. The need to eat can be expressed in as many ways as there are individuals. Whether it took thousands, or just hundreds of generations, eating became more that just satisfying the fundamental need to nourish.

What happens to people with food allergies? The fundamental need still exists however people with allergies will be limited in the foods they can eat. The limit is not imposed from outside, but as a result of the consequences of eating inappropriate foods. Children learn they are lactose intolerant, or have a peanut allergy. Those foods are kept from their range of possible acts. But even these types of situations stimulate thought and actions. Soy milk and lactose free milks were developed and made available, increasing the knowledge base of possible foods for all humans. Individuals have taken the knowledge of food and allergies and applied different preparations and in the process added to the knowledge and range of expressed actions that constitutes the human condition.

As humans gain new knowledge and combine it with the existing base, we innovate. We think new thoughts and each new thought needs new actions to express it. There is an infinite range of thoughts. The range of actions needed to express those thoughts is equally infinite. Each action awaits someone to imagine it and to consider acting in that specific way. Until someone does, the action remains unknown. Until the first person sang, there was no singing. Until the first person danced, there was no dancing. As knowledge spreads, actions spread.

Many of our actions are part of the human condition. They exist in every society and from archeology we can find evidence of many common actions in every grouping of humans from the earliest history. For many actions, their first expression resides tens (or even hundreds) of thousands of years in the past. Many more actions await our imagination in the future. The universe of known actions continues to grow with each succeeding generation.

The source of every thought and action is the individual. An individual, using their knowledge, experience and thought, considered an action and expressed it. Every thought and action finds its source in the individual. Every expression of an action is by individuals, either solely or with the assent or joining of others.

Limits by Self: Consequences, free will

The abilities and resources of the individual naturally limit the free expression of an action. Limits can also be self-imposed by the individual. All actions have consequences. When an action has been expressed for a long time, the consequences of its expression are well known. Often those consequences are precisely the intent of our action. Over history the expression of certain actions has resulted in specific consequences so consistently that the action and its consequences are tightly correlated. If this is the result you seek, this is the action you take. If this is the action you take, this is the result. Further, if the consequence of a specific action satisfies a need of the human condition, the action associated with it becomes fundamental to our behavior. Consider procreation.

However, new thoughts often require new actions that might have poorly understood consequences. If each human can express an action to the limit of their abilities and resources, the effects of those actions can extend and potentially threaten the free expression of other individuals. When this happens and the people know each other, it is possible for them to work together to either minimize the impact, or share the consequences. Individuals can choose to limit their actions to the extent that the consequences of their actions do not extend to the others. This self-limitation helps individuals function in groups or society.

The action continues to exist but a limitation has been imposed upon its free expression. The individual on the other side of the fire will bash my head in if I attempt to express my desire for his spouse. I can still act, if I am willing to live with the consequences. The learning curve for such self-limitation was probably pretty steep but those that survived the process passed along that knowledge along with the knowledge of the act itself.

Over time the consequences associated with particular actions became well understood, yet there remain inherent dangers not only to the individual, but also to those around him or her. The limits of the individual's abilities and resources reduces the risks to others, but most individuals will impose additional limits on the free expression of their own actions in order to obtain the consequences they seek. Within a range of behaviors where consequences are well known and defined, individual actions with limits of expression become the established norm, or tradition.

When acts are rights

To this point, we have talked about how thoughts originate and are owned and controlled by the individual. Thoughts expressed outwardly by actions that support fundamental needs (essential to the continued existence of the individual) are part of the human condition that we share with every individual. These actions are the foundation of rights. A right is the individual ability and freedom to express a thought through action.

An inalienable right is the individual ability and freedom to express a thought through action that satisfies a fundamental need. You can not deprive the individual of the freedom to take these actions without depriving the individual of those needs required to continue to exist. Deprive individuals of the freedom to satisfy fundamental needs and you are a threat to the existence of ALL that share the human condition.

Yet, not all rights are inalienable. Beneficial acts are rights to the extent they ensure, assist, improve or satisfy the needs of the human condition. I must have the freedom to obtain food in order to satisfy the inalienable right to eat. The right however is limited to actions that do not threaten the freedom of others. I can also assign beneficial acts to be done by others. I can authorize the state to provide for my protection (self-defense). I can hire a cook to obtain and prepare food.

Rights exist because we have the need to express thoughts fundamental to our existence. We assert the freedom to express

41

those fundamental acts. We assert the freedom to satisfy our needs. The historical source of our rights is not some government or document, but in the human need, freedom, and ability to express thoughts by action. I am not granted a right; a right is an assertion of the individual ability and freedom to act.

Every right finds its source in the individual. The freedom to act is not a function of society; it is part of the foundation of the human condition, to live, to exist. From your first expression of free will, you have the freedom to act to satisfy the needs of the human condition. Consider:

> Unfortunately, not everyone has the abilities or resources to express every act. This does not deny them the action, they lack the ability to express it. Every action has natural limits. Actions we express are limited by our imagination, our abilities and the resources we have available. We also impose limits ourselves as we learn the consequences of our actions and finally, if we wish to participate in society, whether that is just one other person, or millions, we chose to place limits on our actions in order to improve our situations.

> Unfortunately, not everyone has the abilities or resources to express every right. This does not deny them the right, they lack the ability to express it. Every right has natural limits. Rights we express are limited by our imagination, our abilities and the resources we have available. We also impose limits ourselves as we learn the consequences of our actions and finally, if we wish to participate in society, whether that is just one other person, or millions, we chose to place limits on our rights in order to improve our situations.

Rights are dependent upon our freedom and abilities. I do not have the right to jump ten feet into the air because I lack the ability to jump ten feet into the air. I do not have the right to sing if I lack vocal cords. I have no right to life if my heart ceases to beat.

If my life is mine, not just to live, but to do as I chose with it, then liberty is that freedom of action. On the Island, without exception, every action you took was either to further your survival or increase the comfort of your situation.

Joining with others in society is a beneficial act. How much you limit your actions for that survival and comfort is both an indicator of the value of the society you belong to and the value of your contribution to it.

Not every act will be fundamental or beneficial. Evil acts are those actions calculated to deprive others of their freedoms to express their thoughts or deprive them of the ability to satisfy the needs of their human condition. While an act that threatens others could satisfy a fundamental need, the act itself creates in others the fundamental need to stop it. This defines the limit of a right: actions that satisfy a part of the human condition can not threaten other humans.

Each human has needs that must be fulfilled and as long as each can fulfill those needs, there is no cause to interfere with anyone else's actions. In early human history, our planet offered abundant resources and virtually unlimited space. Humans formed small groups to increase the available resources (hands and brains) and to accomplish more than one or two could do themselves (bringing down a large animal). As long as each individual was allowed to fulfill their needs, the social groupings were beneficial.

For those early societies, a human that took the needs from another was no different than a beast attempting to attack a human and was probably treated no differently, either running him off or beating and leaving behind. From these early beginnings we have the concept of property. THIS is mine. THAT is yours.

"Though the earth and all inferior creatures be common to all men, yet every man has a 'property' in his own 'person'.

This nobody has any right to but himself. The 'labour' of his body and the 'work' of his hands, we may say, are properly his. Whatsoever, then, he removes out of the state that Nature hath provided and left it in, he hath mixed his labour with it, and joined to It something that is his own, and thereby makes it is his property.[47]

In general, the following conditions are required in order to justify the right of first occupancy for a given piece of land. First, the land must as yet be uninhabited; secondly, no more must be occupied than is needed for subsistence[48]; and in the third place, possession must be taken not by empty ceremonies, but by work and cultivation, the only mark of ownership which ought, in default of juridical title, to be respected by others."[49]

Items that fulfilled the needs of the human condition were acquired and the effort to do so created ownership. Berries on a bush were available to anyone that came by and picked them. However, once picked, the effort to do so gave the person that picked them greater claim to them. Property is a characteristic of the effort of the individual. Before great societies a piece of land had no owner. The land existed. When someone came upon the land and then put labor to it, they held a claim against the land and against any other. If the land fulfilled a need of the human condition only with the effort of an individual, that individual had a claim on the fruits of his labor that exceeded any others. This is the foundation of private property.

Limits by Force: Individual, Society, Government

"For though they that speak of this subject use to confound jus and lex, right and law, yet they ought to be distinguished, because right consisteth in liberty to do, or to forbear; whereas law determineth and bindeth to one of them: so that law and right differ as much as obligation and liberty, which in one and the same matter are inconsistent."[50]

In the island society, it was mutual agreement that guided choices and actions. But what happens when one breaks that agreement? Such issues on the island must be resolved by the two, but in a society of millions, the mutual agreement that exists is the system of laws that each society creates.

What is the purpose of society or government? Sir William Blackstone (1723-1780):

"The absolute rights of man, considered as a free agent, endowed with discernment to know good from evil, and with power of choosing those measures which appear to him to be most desirable, are usually summed up in one general appellation, and denominated the natural liberty of mankind. This natural liberty consists properly in a power of acting as one thinks fit, without any restraint or control, unless by the law of nature: being a right inherent in us by birth, and one of the gifts of God to man at his creation, when he endued him with the faculty of free will. But every man, when he enters into society, gives up a part of his natural liberty, as the price of so valuable a purchase; and, in consideration of receiving the advantages of mutual commerce, obliges himself to conform to those laws, which the community has thought proper to establish."[51]

"For the principal aim of society is to protect individuals in the enjoyment of those absolute rights, which were vest in them by the immutable laws of nature;"[52]

Society can be a benefit. Its role is to protect the individual's rights. On the island, the society of two exemplifies the benefits: individuals working together for the benefit of both. When a society becomes inimical to the individual then it becomes a greater threat than any dictator does.

Laws do not prevent the actions of their focus; they punish infractions. Those punishments establish consequences that people can use to make choices (such as civil disobedience). However, some punishments carry the penalty of incarceration.

The forcible restriction of liberty is the only limit imposed by others we freely accept as a necessary component for the function of society. The authority for that force is granted by individuals to a government.

Authorities

What is authority? When one or more other individuals have agreed to act in agreement with me, our actions constitute a single right to act that does not exist individually. It allows each individual in the agreement to call upon others in the agreement to act in concert. Its simplest form is created when we enter into a personal relationship with another individual. This is the foundation of marriage. It is an outward declaration that two individuals act as one and have claim on the freedom to act of the other.

Other forms of authority create communities, companies, organizations and governments. We give others the ability to call upon our freedoms either directly or indirectly by agreeing to limit our actions for the benefit of the larger group. Locke called it the social contract.

When we give an individual or organization the ability to exercise a right in our name either for our benefit (such as an attorney) or the benefit of the community (society), we have granted them authority. Our lack of consent revokes or denies the authority to act in our name. This grant of authority is limited as to allowed acts and duration.

Our right to self-defense is an example where we give the State to authority to act in our stead. It has authority because it has our ascent to do so.

Recalling Locke:

> "The power that every individual gave the society when he entered into it can never revert to the individuals again, as long as society lasts, but will always remain in the

community"[53]

Rousseau said basically the same thing - individuals were the source of authority, but once given to society, it could not be repealed or reclaimed. I believe both are wrong. It doesn't happen often, but some societies become so corrupt and destructive to the individual that it undergoes an upheaval that destroys the old structures and replaces them - such was the upheaval of our founding. No less than all the structures of authorities were rendered and replaced; we didn't just reorder and reauthorize anew our government, but our society.

Introduction to Part Two

Originally, this section was part of that online debate. If at times it appears that I am answering a question from the Antagonist, I am. There are other beliefs as to the foundation or origin of rights. The two most common are morality and traditions.

Morality foundations find their support in the idea that God has ordained or prohibited certain behaviors and it is appropriate to make laws for all based on those proclamations. Where God has been quiet, such as privacy, no right exists.

When morality based on religion fails to define rights sufficient to our current period in time, we get argument that tradition and the vast experience of our ancestors defines the full extent of our rights. The position is that our ancestors have tried all the variations and only what is left, works; that our institutions and historical precedent guide the range and extent of rights.

Both foundations or origins fail to move forward with human knowledge and experience. Leprosy is not the corruption of the skin by sin; seizures are not the outward manifestation of the inner battle against demons; fabrics are just clothes; pigs are just another meat that needs careful preparation; gays are natural variations in the human species; and our fathers do not want us to grow up with nothing more than they have or had.

Our rights are more than just the experience of our past, or the limits of our beliefs. They are the infinite expression of our free will.

Part Two: Of Politics and Government

From Federalist #2 author John Jay:

> "Nothing is more certain than the indispensable necessity of government, and it is equally undeniable, that whenever and however it is instituted, the people must cede to it some of their natural rights in order to vest it with requisite powers."

Jay agreed with Locke over the need for government to protect us from ourselves. In my weaker moments, I sometimes agree that we have a long way to go to maturity. However, I am not willing to give government control over my liberty where others are not threatened. Government is a tool of society and society has, as Mill indicated, a tendency to put itself above the individual.

The most basic component of society is the individual, not the state, or the community, nor even the family. Some may argue that it takes a village to raise a child, but only when individuals are free to interact do we have a viable society. Society would not exist without the individual and the freedom of that individual to associate with others.

One individual does not make a society. Build a structure that divides two people such that neither can interact with the other, and society does not arise separately on both sides of the divide. Only when two or more individuals interact do we see the beginnings of family, community, village or society. How we interact gives structure and definition to the groupings that arise. If these groupings are to survive, they must function to protect the individual's ability and freedom to interact. Society then must protect the individual and the individual's ability and freedom to interact with others.

The human construct, society, serves many of the same purposes as 'species' does in nature. Society seeks to perpetuate itself, to encourage individuals to carry the load of continuing society into the future. Society imposes limitations on individuals so they conform to the needs of the society, at the expense of the individual's liberty. Society uses morality to create a framework for competition to fulfill its needs.

Morality Foundations

Hobbes, Locke, Rousseau and Jay all concluded that without some threat overhanging human choice, humans would be 'at war' with each other forever. Even a casual review of human history shows that the 'threat' used for the last couple of millennium caused as much or more war than it prevented. Society has created large populations operating under the same (and competing) rules. Maybe I am guilty of the same confusion Paine noted – confusing society and government.

Society is interested in perpetuating the species; its goal is to manage humanity. Society uses government to establish its morality as law. If society oversteps its authority informally, what damage can it do? When its morality become laws individuals must adhere to under threat, those threats can interfere with fundamental acts. Society is slow to change, but no formal structures prevent it; government doesn't tolerate the incremental, informal changes that characterize human behaviors. To paraphrase Mill, the best government interferes least.

Our rights, inherent in our creation, are not based in society's good graces, considered permission, disgusted acceptance, or moral acquiescence.

> The concept of natural rights is absolutely dependent on morality. Without them, we have no rights of any kind and life would be "nasty, brutish, and short".

I disagreed with this during the debate and do so again. The implied premise is that our rights are the result of others allowing us to have them. That without other people to grant/protect/sanction our rights, they would not exist. The basis for that grant/protection/ sanction has several different foundations.

From the Stanford Encyclopedia of Philosophy[54], the term "morality" can be used either

1. descriptively to refer to a code of conduct put forward by a society or,

   i. Some other group, such as a religion, or

   ii. Accepted by an individual for her own behavior

or,

2. normatively to refer to a code of conduct that, given specified conditions, would be put forward by all rational persons.

What society proclaims, society can therefore deny. Edmund Burke thought that liberty was worthless unless it was combined with:

> "…government, with public force, with the discipline and obedience of armies, with the collection of an effective and well-distributed revenue, with morality and religion, with the solidity of property, with peace and order, with civil and social manners."[55]

His concept of ordered liberty, so often espoused today, had a flavor many might actually find bitter:

> "You would have rendered the cause of liberty venerable in the eyes of every worthy mind in every nation. You would have shamed despotism from the earth, by showing that freedom was not only reconcilable, but, as when well disciplined it is, auxiliary to law. You would have had an unoppressive but a productive revenue. You would have had a flourishing commerce to feed it. You would have had a free constitution; a potent monarchy; a disciplined army; a reformed and venerated clergy; a mitigated but spirited nobility, to lead your virtue, not to overlay it; you would

51

have had a liberal order of commons, to emulate and to recruit that nobility; **you would have had a protected, satisfied, laborious, and obedient people**, taught to seek and to recognise the happiness that is to be found by virtue in all conditions; in which consists the true moral equality of mankind, and not in that monstrous fiction, which, by **inspiring false ideas and vain expectations** into men destined to travel in the obscure walk of laborious life, serves only to aggravate and embitter that real inequality, which it never can remove; and which the order of civil life establishes as much for the benefit of those whom it must leave in an humble state, as those whom it is able to exalt to a condition more splendid, but not more happy."[56]**(bolds mine)**

Protected, satisfied, laborious and obedient people…not exactly the vision of our founding. Freedom is messy. Ordered liberty is first, predictable but foremost, confining. Ordered liberty is everyone and everything in its proper place. It is the enslavement of the soul.

Further, the "inspiring false ideas" he considers a monstrous fiction is that all men are created equal. Burke argues that some are destined to serve and some are destined to lead and inspiring some to exceed their station is to leave them angry and bitter when it can not happen. Burke's support of the American Revolution was safe – far in distance and time (months of ship travel) from his comfortable life. The Revolution in France struck too close to home and threatened his own station.

Morality is a system of behavior or rules humans' use as a species to maintain control over individuals. In general, moral behavior is defined as either what "God" wants or what benefits humanity as a whole[57]. Neither definition encompasses what the individual wants or needs.

Morality imposed is tyranny. That does not mean morality is bad. Morality is any system of behavior that has rules and structure. Even pirates and thieves have a morality. There are several codes of conduct that can establish a moral society:

Sparta had a code of conduct most found brutal and yet functioned for their society. Sharia law is a code of conduct some suggest (rightly) that is incompatible with democracy or liberty. Communism, socialism, fascism and despotism all have codes of conduct that deny the individual liberty.

Let me note that our country was founded by a deeply religious people. The vast majority were Christians of one form or another. But despite this foundation, they determined our government would not benefit or harm faith or religion. President Obama once claimed we are not a Christian nation – he was wrong. Every aspect of our founding is predicated on the concept that its citizens followed a moral path, predominantly Christian. To deny our history is to establish a false premise – that our Founders abhorred morality. Nothing could be further from the truth. It is clear that Judeo-Christian ethics first guided our Founders, then compelled them to honor those ethics by protecting everyone from the tyranny of allowing government to enforce them.

Religious Morality

"We have staked the whole future of American civilization, not upon the power of government, far from it. We've staked the future of all our political institutions upon our capacity…to sustain ourselves according to the Ten Commandments of God."

James Madison

Madison does not state we based the foundation of our government on the Ten Commandments, but that we as citizens would live according to them. It is the idea that our government, unable to enforce a morality, must rely on a 'moral' people to behave appropriately. If people choose to follow a Christian morality for their own behavior, their friends, neighbors and fellows will benefit from doing so.

The Ten Commandments:
> 1. *You shall have no other gods before me*
> 2. *You shall not make for yourself any carved image, or any likeness of anything that is in heaven above, or that is in the earth beneath, or that is in the water under the earth; you shall not bow down to them nor serve them*
> 3. *You shall not take the name of the Lord your God in vain*
> 4. *Remember the Sabbath day, to keep it holy*
> 5. *Honor your father and your mother*
> 6. *You shall not murder*
> 7. *You shall not commit adultery*
> 8. *You shall not steal*
> 9. *You shall not bear false witness against your neighbor*
> 10. *You shall not covet your neighbor's house*

Should society establish a formal rule (law) to codify each Commandment? What benefit does society expect from doing so? The first four deal with the individual relationship with God. Do we want laws about which God to honor/worship? About icon creation? About swearing? Which day do we want to keep holy, Saturday or Sunday and do we want thought police checking married individuals for inappropriate thinking about neighbors?

Each of these Commandments might be useful guidelines within a religious community but not as a foundation for a diverse population and not one based on the principles of individual liberty. Ignoring those, we are left with the four (slightly out of order) Commandments that deal with how we interact as individuals.

#6: You shall not murder. This is the same as Hobbes' and Locke's consequence of nature/reason. People can and do murder. The Commandment, like any law, acknowledges the ability to act and yet does not prevent it.

#8: You shall not steal. Some societies are brutal with thieves. In the days of Moses, there were few if any luxuries; possessions were necessary for survival. Depriving another of his needs or property constitutes a threat to the individual and his family.

#9: You shall not bear false witness. In early societies there were no 30-page contracts; a man's word formed the covenants and agreements he was expected to honor. However, Hobbes and Locke both felt that honoring those covenants needed the threat of eternal damnation to enforce them. Speaking falsely left others no options but to cease dealing with the liar. In today's society, the white lie is practically a necessity (but much less necessary than most think). The need for honest agreements exists in all communities and a more immediate consequence is needed than some future damnation threat.

#7: You shall not commit adultery. Here we have a personal covenant; dishonor here disrupts the family – the first level of society. Do we want society to intrude into personal relationships? Do we want courts deciding punishment for failure to keep sacraments? Society may have an interest in the relationship, but government does not. Government has become involved due to the nature of secular contracts (of which marriage has become), but adjudicating? Imposing a continuation of the marriage contract exceeds society's interest in the relationship (as it is unlikely to continue to serve the interests of society).

If society has the requirement to protect the individual ability to freely associate with others then any formal rules must conform to that requirement. Compelling specific performance of personal relationships interferes with that requirement.

Forcing a chosen morality upon others is what Madison and the Founders sought to avoid. Catholics, Calvinists and others have different moral precepts and to attempt to enforce one on others is a religious tyranny the original Colonists fled from. That impulse, for religious freedom, became part of 'genetic' makeup of the country and was expressed in the Declaration of Independence.

Traditional Foundations

Suggesting tradition forms a basis for rights resurrects the dead

– or at least their reason. If that is the basis for law or rights, then why bother with rights at all. Slaves can continue to serve; races can continue to segregate; men can continue to rape; women can continue as chattel.

Edmund Burke sought to place a limit on individual freedom by tradition or proclamation in the sense that a statement uttered centuries ago would be binding:

> "To provide for these objects, and therefore to exclude for ever the Old Jewry doctrine of "a right to choose our own governors," they follow with a clause containing a most solemn pledge, taken from the preceding act of Queen Elizabeth, as solemn a pledge as ever was or can be given in favour of an hereditary succession, and as solemn a renunciation as could be made of the principles by this Society imputed to them. "The Lords spiritual and temporal, and Commons, do, in the name of all the people aforesaid, most humbly and faithfully submit themselves, their heirs and posterities for ever; and do faithfully promise that they will stand to maintain, and defend their said Majesties, and also the limitation of the crown, herein specified and contained, to the utmost of their powers," [58]

> "So far is it from being true, that we acquired a right by the Revolution to elect our kings, that if we had possessed it before, the English nation did at that time most solemnly renounce and abdicate it, for themselves, and for all their posterity for ever."[59]

Thomas Paine refutes Burke and the idea that the past can dictate to the future:

> "Every age and generation must be as free to act for itself in all cases as the age and generations which preceded it. The vanity and presumption of governing beyond the grave is the most ridiculous and insolent of all tyrannies. Man has no property in man; neither has any generation a property in the

generations which are to follow. Every generation is, and must be, competent to all the purposes which its occasions require. It is the living, and not the dead that are to be accommodated. When man ceases to be, his power and his wants cease with him; and having no longer any participation in the concerns of this world, he has no longer any authority in directing who shall be its governors, or how its government shall be organised, or how administered."[60]

"Those who have quitted the world, and those who have not yet arrived at it, are as remote from each other as the utmost stretch of mortal imagination can conceive. What possible obligation, then, can exist between them- what rule or principle can be laid down that of two nonentities, the one out of existence and the other not in, and who never can meet in this world, the one should control the other to the end of time?"[61]

"The circumstances of the world are continually changing, and the opinions of men change also; and as government is for the living, and not for the dead, it is the living only that has any right in it. That which may be thought right and found convenient in one age may be thought wrong and found inconvenient in another. In such cases, who is to decide, the living or the dead?"[62]

Burke wanted to bind all posterity using the oath of the long dead. Do I want to be bound by the oaths of my father? Or mother? Did they intend that I should be? Traditions and the past have a venerated spot in our lives, but not in our laws. Traditions HONOR our past; they remind us of the struggles and achievements of our ancestors. Celebrate them, but don't make them into chains or undying covenants.

Sovereign (Rights) Foundations

Morality defines what is right and wrong, but it is not just a sterile list from thousands of years ago. There is a foundation to right and wrong. It should be clear that "right" and "wrong" are based on acts that affect others.[63] Too often that foundation is lost and the reason why something was right or wrong is also lost.

When a morality protects the individual it provides a foundation for a beneficial society. When a morality places the individual somewhere below society, or groups, it is corrupt. The individual is not a disposable piece.

Consider the individual. What does the individual own that is uniquely his/hers? And those 'things' that are owned, are there any that can only be owned by a single individual and no others? We have started with thoughts. Each belongs uniquely to the individual that holds them. They are inalienable. They exist in each of us but can not be 'taken' by another to increase their thought – you may only be deprived of the ability to have/hold thought (by death).

We each have our own life. I can not take your life and add to my own. Stealing a dollar from you increases my wealth and decreases yours, but taking your life does not increase my, or anyone else's life. This ownership of one's life is indicative of individual sovereignty. Only the individual that owns their life can benefit from it. They may use the fruits of that life to benefit others, but no other may take and benefit from your life, they may only deprive you of it.

Our labors likewise are unique to each individual. I can not take your labor and add to my ability to labor. While the fruits of your labor can be taken, sold, or acquired, the labor itself is beyond the reach of others except as to deprive you of your ability.

This ownership is one characteristic of inalienable rights. Deprive me of speech and it does not increase your ability to speak; deprive me of breath and it does not increase your ability to breathe. If you deprive Tiger Woods the ability to play golf, it will not make you a golfer of his caliber. If you deprive Michael Jordan the ability to play basketball it will not allow you to jump higher. The inherent right can not be

58

assigned, transferred or acquired by another. You may deprive another of the action, but you can not add to your own right by doing so.

If there is no individual benefit from depriving individuals of rights, is there a species/societal benefit from doing so? It could be argued in a period of scarcity that fewer individuals would allow for increased resources for the remainder. The taking of the lives of some would increase the 'liberty' of others. The question that would be asked is which individuals would be 'sacrificed' and which would remain?

Society could argue that for the greater benefit, individuals would be deprived of their rights. Many have made the argument "for the greater good" and the result has been murderous tyrannies for a century.

Society may take my life and snuff it out without so much as a glance if that is its choice. However, our Founding was based on the idea that rights are inherent and that without cause, society had no right to infringe upon them...with an exception:

> "What principle is, that the sole end for which mankind are warranted, individually or collectively in interfering with the liberty of action of any of their number, is self-protection. That the only purpose for which power can be rightfully exercised over any member of a civilized community, against his will, is to prevent harm to others. His own good, either physical or moral, is not a sufficient warrant. He cannot rightfully be compelled to do or forbear because it will be better for him to do so, because it will make him happier, because, in the opinions of others, to do so would be wise, or even right. These are good reasons for remonstrating with him, or reasoning with him, or persuading him, or entreating him, but not for compelling him, or visiting him with any evil, in case he do otherwise. To justify that, the conduct from which it is desired to deter him must be calculated to produce evil to some one else."[64]

The individual is sovereign. The state and society are allowed some authority over us as acknowledgment that each of our fellow citizens has an equal position of sovereignty.

Society attempts to limit the free expression of my rights by the laws it establishes. The suggestion that a moral code is the basis for rights risks the elimination of rights should the moral code change. Such is the nasty, brutish and short life of women under the moral code of Islam. Rights exist absent any morality, law or Constitution.

> *You claim that there is no direct relationship between morality and rights*

No direct relationship in their existence; any code that formalizes the state of nature just replaces the need for all to reason for themselves. But the code only recognizes what already exists in nature. Such a generally accepted code aids in their free expression. Rights exist. Living alone on a deserted island, they exist. There, I have a free and unfettered ability to express thoughts as I choose. My sovereignty has no bounds except the limits of the shore (and a small distance beyond).

However, we do not live on a deserted island. We must give up some freedom to express rights in order to have a civil society. I am sovereign, but so is my neighbor, such is the state of nature "equal and independent". We each give up some freedom to live neighborly. But our society is bigger than our neighborhood and we can't rely on the moral code of those that live far removed, so laws are created that establish the limits on our free expression of rights and allow us to enforce those limits on others with a different moral code than ours. The moral code becomes irrelevant. Laws establish a limit on everyone's free expression of their rights.

Your moral code doesn't matter, my moral code doesn't matter, the law reflects the limit to which we both are willing to infringe upon the free expression of our rights. A third moral code introduced into the mix becomes an interesting, but irrelevant issue. The law is based upon our agreement to give up a portion of our rights. If the third moral code demands we give up more, it can go to hell.

But if our rights are based upon the moral code of the majority of society formalized in laws, then a change in majority can demand, and get, a change in our rights. The reason I never considered visiting the Middle East is their moral code is a death sentence to me. Fortunately our laws are not based in a morality, but in inherent rights.

YOU may have a moral code. YOU may use such a code to justify supporting a law. BUT, the law, if based on a moral code, can be changed to reflect new moral codes. YOUR moral code, enacted into law, punishes you for rape. Someone else's moral code, should a community large enough and stable enough to decide so, can be made into law that would eliminate the ability of any woman to accuse you of rape.

Moral codes can make bad laws. They certainly can be used to support the status quo and stifle change. Moral codes supported slavery, supported the prevention of interracial marriage, supported the denial of voting to women, and supported women as chattel.

What is a moral? It is defined as relating to principles of right and wrong in behavior. What is right and wrong in behavior? Is it wrong to kill someone? What if it is a murderer? Or Hitler, whom as far as I know never actually killed anyone. I would argue that it is wrong to deprive someone of their rights and that a system or code of behavior designed to protect the rights of the individual would be superior to a code of behavior that marginalized or denied the rights of the individual.[65]

And by the way, you do NOT have a "right" to dance.

Yea, I do. Nothing on this green Earth except my own capabilities can prevent me from the free exercise of my right to dance. Nothing. Excuse me a sec....

whew SEETHUMA!

Whether you believe our inherent rights are endowed by the Creator, or natural to our existence, it doesn't matter. What is the phrase: you may not believe in God, but He believes in you. I may not believe in God, but my rights don't require it.

Sovereignty of the Individual

The Founders believed that our natural rights as humans came from somewhere for some reason - you believe they came from nowhere for no reason, but just exist.

Our rights are founded on the requirement that individuals must act to satisfy fundamental needs to continue to exist. Whether God exists or not, our needs do.

"Under the law of nature, all men are born free, every one comes into the world with a right to his own person, which includes the liberty of moving and using it at his own will. This is what is called personal liberty, and is given him by the Author of nature, because necessary for his own sustenance." [66]
--Thomas Jefferson: Legal Argument, 1770

I stand by my position: the individual is sovereign; all rights are inherent in each of our own existence - which absent a society, a Constitution or even God, my rights exist as long as I exist. Society, by laws and imposition of morality, infringe upon those rights.

"Of liberty I would say that, in the whole plenitude of its extent, it is unobstructed action according to our will. But rightful liberty is unobstructed action according to our will within limits drawn around us by the equal rights of others. I do not add 'within the limits of the law,' because law is often but the tyrant's will, and always so when it violates the right of an individual." [67]
--Thomas Jefferson to Isaac H. Tiffany, 1819

All rights are above the law[68]. In a civil society, individuals surrender that portion of their rights, and only that portion, necessary for the orderly function of society. Laws are the agreed upon infringement of society into the free expression of our rights.

My right to liberty can not be used to interfere in the liberty of others. Each citizen, each person, has this liberty. Consider each of us in our own little bubble, free to walk where ever we choose, but limited when we bump into another bubble on the path they have chosen.

Our rights are not dependent upon others. To accept fully that 'all men are created equal' and that each of them are 'endowed by their Creator' means every individual must allow others the freedom to act in ways we can not or choose not to; That each of us individually is fully free to act, fully sovereign. When others refuse to acknowledge the existence of the rights of others – the freedom to satisfy fundamental and beneficial needs – they become a threat to all individuals.

The Founding of the United States of America

A right is the freedom and ability to express a thought through action. There are natural limits, physical limits and self imposed limits to rights. There are restrictions to rights necessary for the functioning of beneficial societies. But a fundamental act that satisfies a fundamental need is an inalienable right. Beneficial acts are rights, inalienable to the extent they ensure, assist, improve or satisfy the needs of the human condition. This is the basis of liberty and the pursuit of happiness. Not all acts are rights. Those acts that seek to take or deprive others of their freedom to express their thoughts for their own gain or pleasures are evil and all individuals have the obligation to prevent such acts.

What is your basis for divining whether a particular assertion of a "right" is correct?

This is the wrong question. The right question is "what is your basis for determining whether a right is fundamental and therefore inalienable, beneficial and therefore subject to some interference by others, or evil and therefore subject to force to prevent or punish the free exercise thereof?" The question goes a long way towards answering itself.

> *If Tracy can conceive of an action, and Tracy thinks they don't infringe or reasonably could be thought to infringe, then Tracy has a right. Nice objective test. It rewards the creative person who is unreasonable. In contrast, a person who is very reasonable but not creative has minimal rights.*

The two problems are 'who gets to decide' and what happens when someone is incapable of acting specifically. The Antagonist suggests that someone has the authority to decide what actions an individual can take BEFORE they act. The implication is that SOMEONE other than the individual has the authority to make such a judgment! Who? The government? Society? Because someone CHOOSES not to carry a firearm doesn't mean they lack the right to do so.

> *Your formulation actually contradicts the Declaration of Independence. Your ability to conceive can be much more creative than someone elses, which means under your test, you would have more "rights" and thus **your "rights" would not be created equal** as specified by the Declaration of Independence.*

Look at the bold portion of that sentence again. There is no equality of ability, or of outcome. There is no equality of acts. We all lack some abilities and therefore are unable to express certain acts. It is the freedom to express our free will that we all share, that is the gift we are endowed with. Some will be able to act in ways others can not; it is not the purpose of government to 'balance' or 'equalize' rights.

"Doctor, after the surgery, will I be able to play the piano?"

"Of course!"
"Great! I always wanted to be able to play!"

The patient always had the freedom to play, but lacking the ability was never able to do so. The freedom was not denied or withheld from the patient. Nor did the doctor 'endow' the patient with the freedom during surgery! We are endowed with the freedom to act. That freedom along with ability and resources allows us express our thoughts through action. Those actions are ours, they belong to us individually and to all other individuals in the human condition.

Some worry that such a definition gives license to anyone to assert anything as a right. There is some basis for the concern. I claim that any act that I can think of, that I have the ability and resources to express and does not interfere with others is a right. But any act that I can think of that requires another person to accomplish does not fit that definition.

I don't have a right to have sex with someone. I don't have a right to make you act in a way favorable to me. I don't have the right to make you act in ways that make me feel more comfortable. Other individuals have their freedom and only when they ascent to act in agreement with me, do my acts have authority over others.

I spoke earlier of authorities:

> When one or more other individuals have agreed to act in agreement with me, our actions constitute a single right to act that does not exist individually.

When we as a society agree to limit our actions for the benefit of all, we grant authority to society to 'enforce' the agreement, usually by forming governments with the power to do so. Governments propose and enact laws to formally establish the limits of our acts for the benefit of all.

Laws are not preventative – they establish consequences. Each law seeks to engage in each of the three limits on rights:

Laws restrict access to resources (nature)
Laws establish consequences (self)
Laws establish punishment (force)

What they don't do is eliminate rights.[69] My ability to kill[70] is not prevented by laws regarding murder – the law does not impede my action – otherwise, "Thou shall not kill" would have been the last word on the act.

If you murder someone you have deprived him or her of the freedom to express thoughts though actions. Murder is a threat to all individuals and each has the RIGHT to use force to prevent. The right to use force against one that would murder belongs to each human. We can give the authority to act on our behalf to another or to a society or to a government to act for us against such individuals that may engage in such threatening acts.

Governments are formed by groups of individuals that design the parameters of government and give it the authority to act. At no point does government appear spontaneously and give individuals the freedom to act. First individuals, then groups, then society THEN government.

To the extent our freedom is protected by the power of society and government, it is restricted by the same power. When the society or government power exceeds what is needed to protect our rights, the restrictions imposed on individuals become tyranny.

For the United States, our Founders laid out the problems with the existing government in the Declaration of Independence and then set about trying to not repeat the problems they found in other types of government. It was not a process without problems. However, we got it finally and the anti-individual, anti-liberty, monarchists[71] have been fighting it ever since.

Like our liberty, our rights precede government. The Constitution is only a document that creates government. Our rights, liberties and freedom exist whether the Constitution exists or not.

The Constitution SPECIFICALLY addresses this:

Amendment IX

The enumeration in the Constitution, of certain rights, shall not be construed to deny or disparage others retained by the people.

It was discussed by our Founding Fathers[72] that a list of rights included in the Constitution would leave us open to the claim that any right not included did not exist. Our rights are not granted by the Constitution, they are protected by it.

Rousseau believed we gave up our personal sovereignty to give the power to the State to act as a sovereign power over us. Thomas Jefferson and Thomas Paine disagreed in the sense that we as sovereigns retain the power to reclaim that sovereignty given to the State when it has become corrupt and no on longer a servant of our will.

"We hold these truths to be self-evident, that all men are created equal, that they are endowed by their Creator with certain unalienable Rights, that among these are Life, Liberty and the pursuit of Happiness.— That to secure these rights, Governments are instituted among Men, deriving their just powers from the consent of the governed, — That whenever any Form of Government becomes destructive of these ends, it is the Right of the People to alter or to abolish it, and to institute new Government, laying its foundation on such principles and organizing its powers in such form, as to them shall seem most likely to effect their Safety and Happiness."

I am often told that whether I believe in God or not doesn't matter, He believes in me. I appreciate the thought but when certain things are attributed to God, I'd like a little more than just faith or belief to support it. Evil people attribute disasters to God bringing down His wrath on some perceived bad people. Such people offer no evidence that disasters are God induced; it would seem to me that the only God induced disaster in history (of Scripture) was the Flood. And God owned up to it and promised not to let it happen again.

When Thomas Jefferson wrote the Declaration of Independence, God/Creator was the only explanation for much of the natural world. As we have grown as a species, we have obtained knowledge and been able to explain much of the natural world in terms that, with respect, displace the need for a God explanation[73].

"We hold these truths to be self-evident"

"These truths" were not self-evident to most people in 1776. Governments were monarchies. Often taken by the sword, rulers were in their positions by Divine Right, or so they claimed. Even those a step or two below the Crown considered the position of the King (and occasionally Queen) the source of individual rights, if rights existed at all.

> "We fear God; we look up with awe to kings; with affection to parliaments; with duty to magistrates; with reverence to priests; and with respect to nobility. Why? Because when such ideas are brought before our minds, it is natural to be so affected; because all other feelings are false and spurious, and tend to corrupt our minds, to vitiate our primary morals, to render us unfit for rational liberty; and by teaching us a servile, licentious, and abandoned insolence, to be our low sport for a few holidays, to make us perfectly fit for, and justly deserving of, slavery, through the whole course of our lives."[74]

Our Declaration of Independence was rightly understood not just a Declaration against England, but against monarchies and all forms of government formed by the sword or fiat. Yet, even to many that opposed England, the idea of a King was too ingrained. Fortunately, George Washington was not one of them.

"that all men are created equal"

A government elected by the people, for the people was as radical a notion as could be imagined.

> "The very idea of the fabrication of a new government is enough to fill us with disgust and horror."[75]

For much of human history, once born, people seldom left their social and economic class. Each group considered their position the result of their birth. No one would suggest that the child born to the King was equal to the child born to the groomsman. By the Declaration, class, in one single act, disappeared, at least in America. Every person born into the United States would share the same human condition, sovereign (except of course slaves).

> "Every measure of prudence, therefore, ought to be assumed for the eventual total extirpation of slavery from the United States.... I have, throughout my whole life, held the practice of slavery in... abhorrence."
> **John Adams, letter to Evans, June 8, 1819**

"that they are endowed by their Creator"

Kings used this concept to justify their rule for thousands of years. THEY were endowed by their Creator to lead and rule. THEY were chosen by GOD to determine the fates of their subjects. Burke ascribed to this notion that each were born to their station and should not be falsely encouraged. Jefferson took the justification of kings and claimed everyone had the right to claim divine justification. No longer would the blessings of the Creator be limited to just the rulers, but to all men. Once more, a simple phrase struck at the heart of the justification of monarchs everywhere.

"with certain unalienable Rights"

Rights? Common men with rights? "By your leave" was a phrase asking permission of the Crown to do, well, everything. Permission to marry, permission to farm, permission to have a child came from the benevolence of the King. Commoners had no rights. Here, we have a country that not only claimed citizens had rights, but that they were unalienable! Not only would citizens not have to ask permission to act, their freedom to act could not be taken away.

If citizens inherently had rights, then they did not require a lord, or king, or even a government to bestow them. And if those rights were already part of the citizen, a lord, king or government could not withdraw them. A government in such a situation would find itself no longer the master of its citizens, but the servant.

"among these are Life, Liberty and the pursuit of Happiness"

How many discussions, essays and books written on these rights, ignore the first words in this partial quote: among these. The list of rights is not limited to these three. Many suggest the idea that all other rights flow from these three. I believe that interpretation is wrong. The phrase is 'among these', it could have been 'foremost among these are...' or, 'first among these are...'. But let us look at the suggestion.

Life first, for whatever follows needs life. There are no rights without life. The dead have no rights. The unborn have no rights[76]. To each of us, when we are born, our lives belong to us, they are not the property of a Crown or a government to call upon.

There is an alternative interpretation: liberty being more important than life, for a life born into bondage is no life at all. If I can never chose my own path, if my happiness will never be a function of my choices, what liberty do I have, what life is that?

What limit is imposed by this freedom of action? Beyond the natural limitations, none. All actions are within my liberty. However, if there is no limit to the number and type of actions, there IS a limit to the scope or range that those actions can reach. My right to liberty can not be used to interfere in the liberty of others. Each citizen, each person, has this liberty.

Government's limits

The right to marry someone of your choosing is not in the Constitution. It simply isn't there. Find a citation for me.

I have no need to find a right in the Constitution for it to exist:

Amendment IX: The enumeration in the Constitution, of certain rights, shall not be construed to deny or disparage others retained by the people.

The Constitution does not grant rights. It restricts them. While people often and continuously claim the Bill of Rights DOES grant rights, an actual reading of them proves otherwise:

* First Amendment – **Congress shall make no law** respecting an establishment of religion, or prohibiting the free exercise thereof; or abridging the freedom of speech, or of the press; or the right of the people peaceably to assemble, and to petition the Government for a redress of grievances.

* Second Amendment – A well regulated Militia being necessary to the security of a free State, **the right of the people to keep and bear arms shall not be infringed**.

* Third Amendment – No Soldier shall, in time of peace be quartered in any house, without the consent of the Owner, nor in time of war, but in a manner to be prescribed by law.

* Fourth Amendment – **The right of the people to be secure** in their persons, houses, papers, and effects, against unreasonable searches and seizures, shall not be violated, and no Warrants shall issue, but upon probable cause, supported by Oath or affirmation, and particularly describing the place to be searched, and the persons or things to be seized.

* Fifth Amendment – **No person shall be held to answer for any capital, or otherwise infamous crime**, unless on a presentment or indictment of a Grand Jury, except in cases arising in the land or naval forces, or in the Militia, when in actual service in time of War or public danger; nor shall any person be subject for the same offense to be twice put in jeopardy of life or limb; nor shall be compelled in any criminal case to be a witness against himself, nor be deprived of life, liberty, or property, without due process of law; nor shall private property be taken for public use, without just compensation.

 * Sixth Amendment – **In all criminal prosecutions, the accused shall enjoy the right[77] to a speedy and public trial**, by an impartial jury of the State and district where in the crime shall have been committed, which district shall have been previously ascertained by law, and to be informed of the nature and cause of the accusation; to be confronted with the witnesses against him; to have compulsory process for obtaining witnesses in his favor, and to have the Assistance of Counsel for his defense.

* Seventh Amendment – In suits at common law, where the value in controversy shall exceed twenty dollars, **the right of trial by jury shall be preserved**, and no fact tried by a jury, shall be otherwise re-examined in any court of the United States, than according to the rules of the common law.

* Eighth Amendment – Excessive bail shall not be required, nor excessive fines imposed, nor cruel and unusual punishments inflicted.

* Ninth Amendment – The enumeration in the Constitution, of certain rights, shall not be construed to deny or disparage others retained by the people.

* Tenth Amendment – The powers not delegated to the United States by the Constitution, nor prohibited by it to the States, are reserved to the States respectively, or to the people.

Each of these put a limit on the actions of the government created by the Constitution; they do not grant rights.

Your logic can be used to justify virtually anything that any person wants to do under the Ninth Amendment.

Claiming a right and the free exercise of that right are TWO very different things. I may have the right to bear arms, but I certainly don't have the right to use them against you "just because I want to". The existence of a right does not preclude a legitimate need of society to infringe upon it, nor does it preclude government's ability to regulate it.

But the right exists without a Constitution to grant it. So, yes, I am using the 9th to suggest that rights exist even if they are not listed - ESPECIALLY - if they are not.

Congress can pass legislation limiting a right, regulating a right, define how that right can be exercised, it can even deny the free expression of a right (though I am very dismayed at the idea). But it can't deny that the right exists, its very action against a right acknowledges its existence. Congress can not make an act illegal without acknowledging that the act exists.

Government can define marriage anyway it wants. It can not deny me the freedom to marry anyone I damn well please - it can however, refuse to provide that marriage with legal

73

protections or benefits. As it has done. The question has never been can; government can do a lot of things it shouldn't do.

Scalia's Dissent in TROXEL et vir. v. GRANVILLE[78]

Does Scalia agree that 9th Amendment includes rights not enumerated?

> "In my view, a right of parents to direct the upbringing of their children is among the "unalienable Rights" with which the Declaration of Independence proclaims "all Men ... are endowed by their Creator." And in my view that right is also among the "othe[r] [rights] retained by the people" which the Ninth Amendment says the Constitution's enumeration of rights "shall not be construed to deny or disparage."

However, defining that right and regulating or restricting it, is not a judicial right:

> "Consequently, while I would think it entirely compatible with the commitment to representative democracy set forth in the founding documents to argue, in legislative chambers or in electoral campaigns, that the state has no power to interfere with parents' authority over the rearing of their children, I do not believe that the power which the Constitution confers upon me as a judge entitles me to deny legal effect to laws that **(in my view)** infringe upon what is **(in my view**) that unenumerated right." **(bolds mine)**

Scalia doesn't think a Judge should be imposing his opinion on the rightness or effect of laws that infringe on a right or should be defining the limits or scope of a right he agrees exists even if not enumerated. I tend to agree with that position.[79]

Scalia acknowledges that rights are inherent, they do not have to be enumerated; that the 9th opens a door in the Constitution for previously unrecognized rights to be introduced to the legal framework established by the Constitution. I believe he is clear in just that portion of the quote, that many rights exist that are not enumerated. He dissented from the majority in that he believed he, as a judge, did not have the right to establish by judicial fiat the legal framework necessary for the expression of a right previously not recognized.

California had created a framework for civil unions that mimicked all the rights/privileges/benefits of marriage, but didn't call it marriage. And that framework for civil unions included gay couples as acceptable participants in the process. The California Supreme Court found that creating civil unions with all the legal framework of marriage but refusing to call it marriage, was an issue of "separate but equal" and that was discrimination. Now, that does not appear to me to be judicial activism; that does not appear to me to be creating a new right out of whole cloth. It appears that two legal frameworks were created legislatively that had all the same attributes, but were not equally applied. I see no judicial interference with legislative process. An argument that the legislature intended two separate but equal frameworks and it should have been left alone I think fails to understand previous rulings against separate but equal frameworks. I could be wrong.

Introduction to Part Three

To recap: the characteristics of the human body have fundamental needs that stimulate thought. These characteristics are the foundation of 'all men are created equal'. Once a thought exists, it is an expression of our free will to hold that thought, dismiss it, expand on it or express that thought by action. Actions taken to satisfy fundamental needs are inalienable – they can not be restricted, surrendered or transferred. Attempts to do so can be met with sufficient force to prevent or stop the attempt. This is the nature of self-defense. We have the obligation and the responsibility to defend ourselves from the attempts of those that seek to deprive individuals of actions necessary to satisfy fundamental needs.

A right is the freedom and ability to express a thought through action. There are natural limits, physical limits and self imposed limits to rights. There are restrictions to rights necessary for the functioning of beneficial societies. But a fundamental act that satisfies a fundamental need is an inalienable right. Beneficial acts are rights to the extent they ensure, assist, improve or satisfy the needs of the human condition. This is the basis of liberty and the pursuit of happiness. Those acts that seek to take or deprive others of their freedom to express their thoughts for their own gains or pleasure are evil and all individuals have the obligation to prevent such acts.

Obligations suggest a moral code and I want to dissuade the reader from thinking along that line. As a member of society, I have given up some of my sovereignty to give authority to the government to act in my stead. But that does not eliminate my responsibilities. Like my rights, my responsibilities do not end because government is involved. I am still responsible to the agreement between myself and my fellow participants in society. Those responsibilities constitute obligations on my part, and yours.

Part Three: Practical Considerations and Consequences

> ...a long habit of not thinking a thing wrong, gives it a
> superficial appearance of being right...

I can conceive of a right that has no means of being expressed
in an objective reality (the right to transfer personal property
from one space station to another without first getting
permission from the space station, HELD, the approval to
transfer includes personal property). Protections on wire-
tapping were not necessary until we actually had wires to tap.
But because there are no means to express a right at a given
time, does not mean it never can, never should be.

Legal rights? The legal framework allowing the expression of a
right does not grant a right. The right exists, the law does not
create it. The law is a regulation of, limiting of, or denial of a
right, not a creation of a right.

Scalia believed there was an unenumerated right, he further
believed that the law infringed upon that right BUT that he had
no right as a judge to impose a legal framework for the free
expression of the right. Which is what he thought their ruling
was doing. He believed, stated, that was the job of the
legislature.

Laws create the framework or boundary for the expression of a
right (you can do this much, but not that way, do it then, but
not over there). The right exists regardless of the law. If there is
no law dealing with seethuma, the right of seethuma still exists.
Laws dealing with seethuma could only regulate or restrict it.

Congress, any government entity, only has the authority we
give it or that we allow it to take from us. The authority it has,
is the authority to infringe upon our rights, not to grant them.

My rights, as inherently endowed, as they exist, give me the
liberty to pursue anything that makes me happy. What they
give YOU is exactly the same freedom. What they DON'T do is

give me license to infringe upon your rights, nor you to infringe on mine.

I can, but do not have the right to, murder because to do so violates, denies the liberty of another. I can take your property but do not have the right to because that denies your right to it. I do not have the right to use my liberty to deny you yours. I can but do not have the right to pursue my happiness at the expense of your liberty to pursue yours.

These rules of conduct, this morality, is based on a system of rights based on the characteristics of the human condition.

I stay my hand not out of a sense of responsibility or morality but out of self-preservation. If I deny you your rights, there is nothing to stay your hand against mine. To threaten you is to expose me to actions of others in your defense.

Just because a judicial result changes the operation of a law, it doesn't automatically mean that a judge is legislating. I will admit, the situations are seldom, and I LIKE the position of Scalia in the dissent I quoted earlier.

We have a right to bear arms. If enough people agree for long enough, we can have a constitutional amendment that denies the expression of that right. We can have a Constitutional amendment that brings back slavery, if enough people agree with it.

This is the danger. If enough people think owning a gun is immoral, then the right can be denied. I do not deny that the morality is justifying the law denying a right, further, in reverse, morality can justify a law recognizing a right. But the right exists regardless. From Mill's On Liberty:

> "Protection, therefore, against the tyranny of the magistrate is not enough; there needs protection also against the tyranny of the prevailing opinion and feeling; against the tendency of society to impose, by other means than civil penalties, its own ideas and practices as rules of conduct on those who dissent from them; to fetter the development, and,

if possible, prevent the formation, of any individuality not in harmony with its ways, and compel all characters to fashion themselves upon the model of its own. There is a limit to the legitimate interference of collective opinion with individual independence; and to find that limit, and maintain it against encroachment, is as indispensable to a good condition of human affairs, as protection against political despotism."

Some can see no other way to build the legal framework for the free expression of liberty. Only our morality provides guidance in the regulation, limit or denial of an inherent right. I disagree.

Endowed by the Creator with certain unalienable rights; does my recognition that you are created, just like me, with unalienable rights constituted a morality? In the sense that morality is a code of conduct, I have a morality that recognizes your rights. Whether you exist or not is irrelevant to my rights. However, that you exist means I recognize you have the same rights that I do. If you don't agree I have rights, others will recognize that you do not and act against you accordingly. Your hand is stayed against me on the basis that you will show yourself untrustworthy to others and risk retribution - not just from me, but also from others[80]. It is self-interest then that stays my hand from the absolute free expression of my rights. I trust that others have the same self-interest but I am willing to use force to protect them.

What is your basis for divining whether a particular assertion of a "right" is correct?

A right is an action taken to satisfy a need of the human condition. The individual, not you, or me, or a committee determines whether the action fulfills a need. The limit of the free expression of that right is the limits of someone else's liberty. The desire to establish some defined package of rights is the tyranny of society - to establish limits on individuals, not of necessity but of preference.

Society seeks to confine individuals into defined and confined boxes. It does not have such authority. That authority rests with the individual.

What is your basis for your "rights as a sovereign."

My rights exist, because I exist. They are necessary for my (our) continued existence. They are inherent. As many will point out, the free expression of those rights can be and is seriously limited by the boundaries of the rights of others.

If I am alone on a deserted island, I have rights. If I don't exist, YOU still have rights. If society didn't exist, they would still exist. Rights do not require 'others' to exist. The right exists, even if I choose NOT to act upon it. My basis recognizes everything. I have lots of rights - society and by it's enforcer, the government - has the authority to punish the expression those rights but it can not deny their existence. Just the attempt to regulate in any way acknowledges the existence of an ability and freedom to act.

A universe of rights exists. A law addresses the interaction of a right exercised by one or more upon the rights of others. A 'new' right has no laws infringing upon it, because no one expected to need such a law.

I used seethuma earlier, let me do so again. If my community sought to establish a law preventing the public display of seethuma and a lower court struck down that law as an unreasonable infringement on my right to seethuma - would you say that the court had created a right where none existed before? Would you say the court had engaged in judicial activism? Some would say the answer is yes to both. If however, the court said the law was too broad and it restricted the public display from 10pm to 8am, would that be judicial activism or creating a right where none existed before? My understanding of Scalia is that he would find the restriction judicial activism because the court created a restriction, not the legislature.

I don't advocate an unfettered freedom to do everything I can conceive of - that is pure libertarianism and anarchy. I do believe there is a universe of rights waiting to be recognized and acted upon. I do believe, once conceived, all rights belong to every individual. They may be limited in their abilities or proclivities to act upon those rights, but they exist nonetheless. Laws establish the limits of those rights; for newly conceived acts, laws don't exist and ANY infringement on them is going to be argued against. This is the foundation of the requirement that our form of government is for a moral people. Government can only react to the consequences of actions not conceived of, once expressed violating someone else's liberty. We rely on the individual expressing a never before conceived of act that they will limit the consequences or protect the liberties of others. The worst, and most useless argument someone can make FOR such infringing laws is that the right proclaimed doesn't exist. It is a stupid, archaic, authoritative position.

Some can argue that a law sufficiently limits/regulates a right to the point that there can be no free exercise of the right without running afoul of the law - therefore there is no legal right but that is just words. The right exists, laws can only punish its expression. It may have no practical difference in your mind, but to the person being denied, it matters.

> *You have the right to an abortion - we are making it*
> *illegal to act upon that right*

is different than

> *You have no right to an abortion; that right does not exist*
> *anywhere in the Constitution and you can't make it up out*
> *of whole cloth.*

In the first case, you need to show a compelling reason why the state can infringe/punish the expression of the right. The second one lets you (the supporters of the denial and the government) off the hook to justify your stance.

Saying that the right doesn't exist or saying that there is no legal right is not justification. You can claim a justification by tradition/status quo, or you can claim a moral position (majority rule), but both of those positions are almost as weak/useless, as claiming no such right exists.

If you want to ban the exercise of a right, fine. Get a majority to agree with you and bam, you can punish anyone that expresses it. Don't call it anything else than an attempt to infringe on individual rights.

My issue has been that attempts to regulate rights are either:

> *the right doesn't exist (in the Constitution, in history, etc.)*

or

> *The right exists, but we are going to deny you the freedom to engage in it.*

I think government has the authority to limit my freedoms to act. It is an authority I have given it as a sovereign, and it may, with the careful scrutiny we have in the Constitution, act against me for the benefit of all that seek to express their rights.

I don't oppose a means of establishing the limits of my freedoms, provided that the means are based in some kind of framework we can agree on. Morality is not one of them. Tradition is not one of them.

The question should not be how do we limit a right, but how much of a right do we have to limit. It is about a point of view, a perspective.

I have the ability to ride a motorcycle without a helmet. How much authority does the government have to punish that ability? Many hate the nanny state because it imposes on our rights, a concept that we can't be adults and accept the consequences of our actions. But defending the status quo is the same thing. Defending the limitation/infringement or denial of a right because, well, it MIGHT have unintended consequences is the same thing as denying us a gun because it MIGHT be used wrongly.

I am asserting a right exists. The basis is: I can conceive it. A right is the ability to act. I have no right to fly into the Sun, notwithstanding Icarus. Maybe, some day, I will own a ship that can fly into the Sun and then we can talk about whether I have the right to do so or not.

But, if I can conceive of an act, I have the right to act in that manner. If in the free expression of that right, my actions infringe upon another, or reasonably could conclude I would, there is an obligation to protect their rights. In the case of seethuma, there are no laws now, so some legal framework might need to be created if I am going to continue to assert the right to seethuma that has the potential to infer in the rights of others.

Such anarchy...people asserting rights no one every heard of before - taking pictures in public...air rights...damn, what will be next? All men are created equal - but that doesn't mean I can dunk a basketball. You have a greater freedom to act than I do, but it has not altered our shared human condition.

The free expression, the acting about that right may be beyond the ability of some, but that does not deny the right for them.

> *If Tracy can conceive of an action, and Tracy thinks they*
> *don't infringe or reasonably could be thought to infringe,*
> *then Tracy has a right.*

And so therefore does anyone else that wishes to repeat the action for themselves. I can not conceive of a right for myself, that excludes by definition anyone else from the free exercise of that same right.

The individual is sovereign. Not, Tracy is (the only) sovereign. In this society, the United States, we have a Constitution that provides the legal framework so that each individual sovereign can freely express his/her liberties to the maximum WITHOUT infringing on others. The only reason government can exercise a limitation upon my free expression of my rights is to protect others.

The individual is sovereign. All rights are inherent in me, as they are in you. I can not freely exercise any right, if in the process, they deny you the ability to freely exercise yours. We give up some of our sovereignty - some of our liberty to freely express our rights, in order to create clearly defined lines where the free expression of our rights can come up to, but not cross. I believe this is the premise that underlies the foundation of the United States.

Individual Interactions

I have the need to breathe – you cannot breathe for me and any purpose you have for denying me breath is subject to my use of force to prevent. There is no right or wrong to breathing, I have the need, I breathe – the absolute freedom/ability to do is "a right". It doesn't require your acknowledgment or acceptance – try to stop me and I will use force against you in order to protect my existence. Others seeing your actions will – if they value their own existence – assist me against you as I would to protect them. This is not a function of society, it is an inherent impulse. We do it as a species.

> *The concept of natural rights is absolutely dependent on morality. Without them, we have no rights of any kind and life would be "nasty, brutish, and short".*

This is one of those beliefs that have become prevalent and wrong. The Antagonist is suggesting that some group – either a religion or community or society – has the ability to determine what rights are appropriate and will be granted or defended; absent this defined set of rights, we have no rights. The position suggests there are no rights when an individual is separated from the group and it is clear such a position is wrong.

I have the need to act in ways that satisfy fundamental needs. Those acts are inalienable rights. You have the same freedom to act to satisfy fundamental needs. If we agree that each have those rights, we can claim there is a moral choice but as we both have the right to defend our acts and selves from others that seek to limit or deprive us of our acts, it is polite babble. The threat of force in defense of our selves is not the establishment of morality in others. It is self-interest.

It is not morality that informs the notion that others have rights, it is reason. However, morality DOES have a purpose. Laws do not prevent evil acts. Our form of government, designed to interfere in personal liberty as little as possible, needs people to act with restraint. We need people to choose to act in ways that maximizes everyone's freedom and those choices constitute a morality.

> "Our Constitution was made only for a moral and religious people. It is wholly inadequate to the government of any other."[81]

The point is that government can not enforce or replace morality in people; it must come from within. Any government that attempts to do so must resort to tyranny at a minimum. With a population committed to self interest and taking all they can for themselves, regardless of the moral or legal issues, they will overwhelm those that act morally or legally or with respect towards others. If they can use the power of government on top of that, we have all the necessary requirements for the type of nightmares we have seen in country after country that have descended into tyranny.

I have said repeatedly that my rights are inherent as your rights are inherent in you. While I respect them, only the threat inherent in their free exercise can ensure that YOU respect them also. You may have that respect for rights, but what of our neighbors, or people in other countries or of other religions? A majority of people can, using our Constitution, re-institute slavery, or return women to a status as chattel. It is our individual responsibility to protect our rights, our ability to fulfill our needs.

I don't believe that society grants rights, I believe that God grants rights. Therefore, while society may deny the practice of natural rights, it cannot take them away.

Free Will

God grants the free will and ability to murder, lie, steal – otherwise, what is the purpose of saying DON'T murder, lie, steal? God says "you can, but don't (or else)"

The Founders believed that our natural rights as humans - something you are understandably focusing on - were granted to us by God,

God gave us free will – the freedom to act. God created the universe – we were inevitable.[82] As much as this will absolutely drive some crazy, you have the 'freedom' to murder. To kill, main, and all the other TERRIBLE things – however, we, individually, have the right to 1) do all in our power to stop you or failing to do so, 2) punish you. There is no law: thou shall not kill. Our laws say WHEN you kill, this is the punishment. If God didn't 'want' us to kill, He could have made such an act impossible. I am NOT SAYING God wants us to kill – but He gave us the ability and freedom to do so and at times commanded humans to kill.[83] Laws do not stop evil acts – otherwise there would be no murders, rapes, thefts, or shootings NOW.

Laws establish two things – the boundary or limit of the consequences of actions, and the punishment for exceeding those boundaries or limits. Laws punish boundary breakers.

You are inviting people to invent rights.

Hell yes! We want people to invent, create, imagine all kinds of new 'rights', new thoughts to express in actions.

Government is a tool, the question should always be asked, is a law or regulation necessary BEFORE asking how much of a law or regulation is necessary. Over time the age of consent for marriage has increased and the prohibition against interracial marriage has ended. Just because tradition has dictated certain outcomes does not mean it should continue to do so – especially if it expands the liberty and freedom of individuals rather than restrict them further.

Your argument can be used to invent all sorts of rights that don't exist:

Why does this sound like there is some list of rights that already exists and that everyone should be limited to? Humanity changes, society changes, technology changes, knowledge changes, why shouldn't the universe of acts change?

According to you, you have a constitutional right to anything except what is prohibited in the Constitution. You should start an Anarchy Party.

The Constitution prohibits GOVERNMENT from certain acts – it neither denies nor allows individuals freedom. The Constitution is all about the limits imposed on government.

Rights can be regulated (punished) but the State must have a compelling reason to interfere with individual liberty. The State can not limit my liberty just because you don't like me doing something (yes, yes....get enough people to vote on it and you can impose any law BUT it will not stop the actions, only create punishments for engaging in them or withdraw resources necessary for them).

A Conversation

The Judiciary only imposes punishment – it can not make or unmake rights. It punishes those that cross established boundaries that the free expression (which it can not in any way limit) of thought should consider when thinking of consequences.

*Laws are rules that cannot be disregarded by society
simply because you feel they are unjust.*

Sure they can, if I'm willing to accept the consequences. But in no way do laws prevent acts like some invisible hand that reaches out and stays an act.

*So anything not listed as a right is automatically included
as a right?*

No list of rights exists anywhere. No one walked up to your parents and handed them a folder upon your birth and proclaimed, "here are the rights your son can exercise".

*You are using Amendment IX like a liberal uses
Amendment XIV.*

The Constitution deals with the behavior of GOVERNMENT, not individuals!

*Your logic can be used to justify virtually anything that
any person wants to do under the Ninth Amendment.*

The Ninth Amendment restricts government from doing things not listed elsewhere.

*There is nothing conservative in your application of
Constitutional law.*

The individual freedom to act is a classical liberal, not statist, position. Historically, the 'conservatives' were monarchists – believers in the authority of the king and state over the individuals.

*Using the 2nd Amendment as an example although it is a
poor one since it is an example of an expressly provided
Constitutional right.*

Wrong. Let's look at the 2nd Amendment:

A well regulated militia being necessary to the security of a free State, the right of the People to keep and bear arms shall not be infringed.

Note it does not grant the right, it says **_government shall not_** **_infringe_** on the right.

> *Congress can (within certain broad limits) pass laws impacting the right to bear arms.*

Yes, well, we do allow for some regulation of rights- the defining and enforcement of boundaries - that are beneficial and certainly those that are evil. However, the first question ANYONE that wishes to propose a law should ask is not how much of a law is appropriate, but whether ANY such law is appropriate.

> *For example, everyone agrees that I can't build a nuclear bomb in my basement.*

I'd say "shouldn't build", but you certainly might be able to do so. Government can do a good job of restricting access to the necessary resources, but you could with the right information and skill.

> *Congress can define to some extent what "arms" means. Congress can also define what "marriage" means. The ability of government (state governments in this case) to define "marriage" has broader latitude than the ability of government to define what "arms" include because there is no Constitutional right to marry the person of your choosing.*
>
> *There are plenty of people I would have chosen to marry, but I have no entitlement to do so.*

You have the freedom to marry whomever you want with their agreement. Government, enforcing a societal dictate, can restrict the recognition of such a marriage and deny equal treatment based on such a restriction, but you still have the freedom to do so.

The use of rights here is the same as boundaries in my formulation. Judges establish boundaries, not rights. The rights exist and nothing judges do can make or unmake them. Judges (referees) do well when they stick to defining the boundaries, not picking the winning team on the field.

> *Scalia does not have the power under the Constitution to deny legal effect to laws even though he thinks they are contrary to the principles on which this country was founded.*

Actually, he and the Supreme Court are charged with that very thing: prevent laws from being enforced that violate the Constitution. I would argue it is their ONLY responsibility. The SCOTUS is the last chance to look at a law or regulation and say: is there a valid government purpose being served?

> *People constantly assert all sorts of "rights" that you would disagree with. In the abstract, "rights" are easy to conceptualize. In the real world, where truly enforceable legal rights impact the enforceable rights of others, it's a lot trickier.*

That is the limit to a right – when it infringes upon the freedom or ability of another. We have reached a point where free will acts as a governor to ourselves. I can kill, but I choose not to. Why? I impose that limit on my actions while reserving the freedom to kill should circumstances warrant the need.

> *No, you don't get it. Recognition of liberty is a moral issue. You have inherent rights because of your existence as a human being. That the Constitution recognizes these rights and seeks to protect them is based on the morality that YOU matter.*

The Constitution restricts government authorities. Ignoring that for the moment, I can choose not to kill you because 1) I have no reason to; 2) you are not a threat to me or others or our freedoms; 3) I am unwilling to deal with the consequences. Each of these reasons could be 'morality' but only number two could be considered a 'principle'. Numbers one and three are free will exercised in a specific situation and subject to change depending on circumstances.

> *Every law is based on morality because, a law is just a governmental enforcement of morality.*

Please, what is the moral precept to a 55mph speed limit? Versus a 65mph speed limit? Laws establish boundaries – the limits of our actions so as to prevent infringement upon the freedoms of others. I'd be interested in the moral basis for no right turn on red.

> *However, Morality (with a big M) does not change. Every law is an extension of perception of Morality. You can separate law from morality, but you cannot have a law without a recognition of (at least a perception of) Morality.*
>
> *WHY is the individual important enough to be protected with laws? Because of their value. THAT is Morality.*

You are putting the carriage before the horse. Laws are a creation of government, which is a creation of society, which is a creation of individuals that seek to work together for their mutual benefit.

You could have a society with no laws if people were capable (someday maybe) of acting with respect towards others. This is the issue 'all at war with each other'. Why? We have the technology now to satisfy the needs of everyone on the planet. We do not now, nor are we every likely to, have the ability to satisfy the wants of everyone. Society benefits individuals when it protects individuals.

When those societies and governments STOP benefiting the individuals, they are subject to dismantling. Laws create

91

boundaries between individuals, they do not assign value. I support a law that infringes upon my rights because I seek the support of others in enforcing boundaries that protect my freedoms. As long as the benefit outweighs the cost, I will continue to do so.

Every law MUST be based on some sort of morality, and if you try to remove one moral set, you only replace it with another.

No right turn on red? Traffic lane designations? Helmet laws? Smoke detector requirements?

You cannot have laws based on 'rights' as the recognition of those rights is a moral stance on the value of the individual. To make laws on 'rights' would require that you ignore the morality upon which the recognition of rights is based.

I have no need to ignore morality, mine or anyone else's to recognize the human condition, that each of us has a need to breathe, to eat, to survive. That recognition could be 'morality', a code of conduct based on the recognition of individual liberty and freedom. It is based on a system of rights – acts necessary for the human condition.

Laws recognize a freedom to act, they imposes a boundary or limit on that act and assign consequences, punishment for exceeding those limits or boundaries. What laws do NOT do is prevent an act.

Upon what basis do you make a law that is amoral (as compared to moral or immoral, but actually NONmoral) but still based on a 'right'? What does such a law even LOOK like? How do you back it up and support it? Upon what does such a law rest? What is its foundation?

Historically, an acre is the amount of land an ox can plow in a day. A law established that an acre is 43,520 square feet.. Zoning ordinances establish property uses and designate parking space sizes and quantities. Ownership of property is a function of our right to the fruits of our labors. The use of that property is infringed by laws that determine specific uses without regard to a 'moral' foundation.

The law establishes a boundary; it does so in a uniform way. I recognize the rights we both have, either of our deaths have no impact on the rights of the other. Whether you or I exist or not is irrelevant to everyone's rights.

Your hand is stayed against me on the basis that you will show yourself untrustworthy to others and risk retribution - not from me, but others.

> *That may be what 'stays your hand', but my hand is stopped from acting against you because I believe you have value as a created being, created by God and loved by God.*

This is a Limit of Self. Your free will exercised. You choose not to act.

> *A test is something that distinguishes between a right from our Creator and a rantings of a lunatic.*

It is not a test that YOU can apply to my actions. Except that my actions might infringe upon yours, your attempt to set limits on my actions is an attempt to deprive me of my freedom. That you do not like some of the actions I take – that have no impact on your own freedom to act – is irrelevant. I have no obligation to accept your judgment whether my actions are acceptable or authorized, or even subject to your opinion.

> *Lunatics can envision a lot. They can act upon it. Your framework can used by tyrants, serial killers, and other madmen to act in some bad ways without limitation.*

Individuals can envision a lot; we can decide whether an act is evil by its impact on the freedoms of others. But acts that do not infringe upon others by definition are not evil; they are

93

beneficial to the individual so acting (otherwise, why would they do so?)[84]. Someone else's pursuit of happiness is not subject to your beliefs or your comfort. As long as acts do not interfere in your (or anyone else's) freedom to act, they are the right of the individual that exercises them.

> *However, to be useful, there has to be a way to put boundaries on person's "rights" versus another person's "rights."*

Finally, a recognition that 'boundaries' are necessary to define the limits of the consequences of actions in order to protect the freedoms of others. Any law must have a compelling reason for the State/Society to justify infringing upon the freedoms of individuals.

> *Just saying there is a universe of rights without providing some type of framework for navigating conflicting claims is for lack of a better word, unhelpful.*
>
> *People have a right to live, but how do you divide up the food.*

Whose food? Food is the fruits of someone's labors. Each of us has a responsibility to fulfill our needs. We do not have the right take or demand from others to do so. Even when a majority using the power of government demand the resources from those that have, it is still an infringement on their freedom.

> *People have a right to shelter, but who builds the place in the first place, and who decides who gets their first choice in rooms.*

A right to the resources necessary for survival is not a claim on the resources and fruits of someone else's labors.

> *People have all sorts of rights, but to be enjoyed, those rights require the exercise of responsibilities.*

There are two sides to rights: the responsibility for the consequences of your acts; and actually acting for your own benefit. Others do not have the responsibility for your survival unless they freely accept it.

> *The fact that we are all sovereign and the existence of a universe of rights is all good and true, BUT IT DOES NOT ACTUALLY HELP DEFINE THE BOUNDARIES OF WHAT BEHAVIOR IS PERMITTED AND WHAT BEHAVIOR IS NOT.*

The acceptable limit of someone's acts is the liberty and freedom of others. Beyond that limit, the pursuit of happiness is not limited to what others think is right or appropriate. You want a way to determine if someone else's act is ok, correct, acceptable, 'moral', BEFORE they act. Why do you have a need for such a method? Who gave you the authority to implement such a system?

We all have the freedom and ability to express all the thoughts we choose to, subject to the boundaries that exist between us.

> *Do you know how many tyrants agreed used your formulation of rights? Tyrants always think of their own conception, and never think their actions are an unreasonable infringement. So your framework gives Stalin, Hitler, Mao, etc. the thumbs up.*

I can express any action, I can exceed the boundaries society has established and yet you think that some categorization of rights changes the dynamic. It does not. I have the freedom and ability to express an infinite range of thoughts, as do you. Whether I think or you think the expression of those thoughts by actions infringe upon others can only impact the exercise of my, or your, free will. We can have all the boundaries in the world, but only the threat of force prevents individuals from ignoring them. When people are either willing to accept the consequences or ignore them for their own pleasure or aggrandizement, we call them or their acts at least, evil. But like acknowledging that drunk drivers abuse the driving privilege but not banning all driving, we need to accept that all actions are the birthright of every individual even when some abuse them.

> *Your arguments would be more persuasive if you tried to create a more objective framework.*
>
> *You shoot down morality (even Ayn Rand would disagree with your use of the morality which even she would acknowledge is equivalent to ethics), but you don't really do anything to define, build up, and explain what a "rights basis" is and how to distinguish between am invalid assertion of a right and a valid assertion of a right.*
>
> *If an analytical framework cannot distinguish between a proper assertion and an improper assertion, it doesn't really accomplish anything.*

You seek someone or something to stand in judgment over what individuals will have the freedom to do. By what authority do you or any Government get to decide how much freedom I should be allowed? That is what you seek – a way to limit my freedom to some defined 'acceptable' actions. Self-defense demands that I respond to such threats will all necessary force to prevent or eliminate your threat to my liberty.

Beyond the requirement that my acts not interfere in the rights of others, there is no framework that says 'this action' an individual can take and 'this action' an individual can not. All actions are possible. The question becomes (and this may be the framework requested), is the action necessary to satisfy the fundamental needs of the human condition? If yes, then it is inalienable – it can not be restricted or denied. A second question can be applied to acts that are beneficial but not fundamental: does it cross a boundary that infringes on another individual's freedom? Rights are not defined by a moral code, only the boundaries between individuals are so established.

For example, the majority of the polity has decided that women have a moral right not to be raped (men, too, for that matter) and have therefore enacted laws prohibiting such acts.

Except the moral majority supported women as chattel and husbands were allowed to 'rape' as their wives were their property and the wife could not deprive them of her body. Morality changes. Further, as has been previously stated, laws do not prohibit acts, they punish acts that exceed boundaries.

Your moral code can be applied to your actions – your free will can be expressed by withholding your actions. But neither you nor I can take a moral code and impose it upon another to use in their considerations. They may embrace such a code, or devise their own, or use reason, or a coin flip. There are many ways to self-limit your actions – but none of them can be imposed by others. Your moral code can justify YOUR choices, but not mine. Of course, you and others can get together and create laws based on your moral code to PUNISH me for acting in ways you find offensive. But it is, and always will be, my choice to act regardless and your infringement upon that freedom.

And by the way, you do NOT have a "right" to dance. Thankfully, Footloose was only a movie but even in real life the polity has the "right" to outlaw dancing.

The majority can enact a law that punishes acts that are rights. The appropriate question is should it? When an act, like dancing, does not impact the freedom to act of others, under what basis does the majority do so? The Constitution, while giving the means, gives no such basis. And a morality that outlaws such acts has no foundation in liberty or individual rights.

The only justification acceptable for infringement/denial (whether that has any impact on the reality of the situation or not) is that the exercise of my right harms others. And that harm has to be objectively shown.

Two Topics

In the online debate and in virtually every discussion about rights that I have had in the last three years, the issues that drove the discussion were gay marriage and abortion.

It was always my argument that individual rights addressed both issues and yet held firm to the principles of our founding. These sections apply my argument to these two topics.

Gay Marriage

The right to marry someone of your choosing is not in the Constitution. It simply isn't there. Find a citation for me.

We covered this extensively, but it still persists that people think there is a list of rights somewhere in the Constitution and if its not listed, it doesn't exist. The following is from Federalist Paper #84 authored by Alexander Hamilton:

> "I go further, and affirm that bills of rights, in the sense and to the extent in which they are contended for, are not only unnecessary in the proposed Constitution, but would even be dangerous."

The full text of #84 is in Appendix A. Please, take a few moments and go read it. I'll wait.

Hmmmm...

seethuma...ah! Back? Good. Moving on.

Withholding the recognition of a legal status is not interference in your personal conduct. There have been laws regulating the privilege that is marriage (there have always been requirements for marriage--going back to before 1789 and such requirements continued past 1789).

There are reasonable limits on contract law imposed by regulations, such as age of consent and unreasonable limits such as no interracial couples.

I have the right to marry whomever I want, I have the right to call it a marriage. The state has the ability to deny legal protections for such a relationship, it has the ability to deny recognition of such a relationship as a marriage. I am simply calling out the position that 'the right to gay marriage doesn't exist in the Constitution' is a useless claim. The right exists, justify denying its exercise based on 'harm'.

Saying a gay marriage harms a straight marriage is insufficient. In the Iowa Supreme Court decision[85] on gay marriage, the Court addressed the issues relating to gay marriage:

Maintaining Traditional Marriage.

Initially, the court considered the County's argument the same-sex marriage ban promotes the "integrity of traditional marriage" by "maintaining the historical and traditional marriage norm ([as] one between a man and a woman)." The court noted that, when tradition is offered as a justification for preserving a statutory scheme challenged on equal protection grounds, the court must determine whether the reasons underlying the tradition are sufficient to satisfy constitutional requirements. These reasons, the court found, must be something other than the preservation of tradition by itself.

"When a certain tradition is used as both the governmental objective and the classification to further that objective, the equal protection analysis is transformed into the circular question of whether the classification accomplishes the governmental objective, which objective is to maintain the classification." Here, the County offered no governmental reason underlying the tradition of limiting marriage to heterosexual couples, so the court proceeded to consider the other reasons advanced by the County for the legislative classification.

Promotion of Optimal Environment to Raise Children.

The second of the County's proffered governmental objectives involves promoting child rearing by a father and a mother in a marital relationship, the optimal milieu according to some social scientists. Although the court found support for the proposition that the interests of children are served equally by same-sex parents and opposite sex parents, it acknowledged the existence of reasoned opinions that dual gender parenting is the optimal environment for children. Nonetheless, the court concluded the classification employed to further that goal—sexual orientation—did not pass intermediate scrutiny because it is significantly under-inclusive and over-inclusive.

The statute, the court found, is under-inclusive because it does not exclude from marriage other groups of parents—such as child abusers, sexual predators, parents neglecting to provide child support, and violent felons—that are undeniably less than optimal parents. If the marriage statute was truly focused on optimal parenting, many classifications of people would be excluded, not merely gay and lesbian people. The statute is also under-inclusive because it does not prohibit same-sex couples from raising children in Iowa. The statute is over-inclusive because not all same-sex couples choose to raise children. The court further noted that the County failed to show how the best interests of children of gay and lesbian parents, who are denied an environment supported by the benefits of marriage under the statute, are served by the ban, or how the ban benefits the interests of children of heterosexual parents. Thus, the court concluded a classification that limits civil marriage to opposite-sex couples is simply not substantially related to the objective of promoting the optimal environment to raise children.

Promotion of Procreation.
Next, the court addressed the County's argument that endorsement of traditional civil marriage will result in more procreation. The court concluded the County's argument is flawed because it fails to address the required analysis of the objective: whether *exclusion* of gay and lesbian individuals from the institution of civil marriage will result in *more* procreation.

The court found no argument to support the conclusion that a goal of additional procreation would be substantially furthered by the exclusion of gays and lesbians from civil marriage.

Promoting Stability in Opposite-Sex Relationships.
The County also asserted that the statute promoted stability in opposite-sex relationships. The court acknowledged that, while the institution of civil marriage likely encourages stability in opposite-sex relationships, there was no evidence to support that *excluding* gay and lesbian people from civil marriage makes opposite-sex marriage more stable.

Some people think of rights as a set of pre-approved acts given to individuals as a package deal like some 'human freedom license' stamped by government. People want to define that package, or have some structure to how the license is used. Rights are your free will expressed. You don't 'lack' a right, your choice not to act doesn't deprive you of the right to do so any more than a comatose patient is 'deprived' of their rights. No laws apply to a comatose patient because they are expressing only the most fundamental acts – breathing, living. Like the parents of a 6-year-old where the parents have assumed the responsibility for satisfying the needs of the child, people assume the responsibility for the comatose patient.

A right is not a license that can be given or/and taken away by some group or organization.

Abortion

My point is that the right to live (the most basic of rights) is aspirational.

"We hold these truths to be self-evident, that all men are created equal, that they are endowed by their Creator with certain unalienable rights, that among these are life, liberty and the pursuit of happiness."

Created, then endowed.

Genesis 2:7 - then the Lord God formed man from the dust of the ground, and breathed into his nostrils the breath of life; and man became a living being.

Formed then breathed life into.

I have stated a process by which rights form and attach to individuals. Rights are acts necessary for the life, liberty and pursuit of happiness of all human individuals. Without thought and free will there are no acts, no rights to be exercised. I do not have the right to do what is not possible. I do not have the right to walk through a wall, or leap over a building.

101

I understand the position of those that oppose abortion. If killing a child one minute after birth is murder, how can killing one minute before birth be any less? And if one minute before birth is murder, why not five minutes, or five hours, or five days, or five months? It is impossible for them to say 'now it is ok to kill, but not one minute from now?' How does humanity draw that line? The pro-life movement refuses to do so.

The Antagonist states that the right to life is aspirational – something to aspire to. He concedes, unwittingly I think, that life is not inherent at the point of conception. I don't aspire to life, I have life and will do all in my power to protect and defend it. But at the point of conception there is no ability to express life. At conception the cell is alive and doing exactly what it is programmed to do.

It is not a matter of perspective, but it is a matter of starting points. Those that oppose abortion start with a right to life and work backwards from that point without seeing how the right ever applies. Their position is that a right to life is always present from the second 'life' begins. But both cells that make up a zygote were alive before joining. Are not those cells deserving of 'life'? Don't they aspire to life? The argument of course is the same one I make, separate there is no potential. Only joined does potential exist but it is only potential, not actual. When the brain dies and the heart stops, there are no rights to be exercised. Before there is a heart to beat and a brain that functions there are no rights to be exercised.

When someone is in a coma, they have no right to speech. They are not being denied speech, or dance. There are no acts to be expressed except life. And if the patient is on machines keeping them alive, there is not even that right. Others may take the responsibility but they can not give the patient life. The mother can take the responsibility to maintain the child but s/he is not capable of it independently. Life is either there to be expressed, or it is not. You can not give what is not in your power to give.

The child in the womb has no rights because s/he lacks the

ability to form a thought and by free will, express that thought through action. Let me qualify that statement. At some point during the pregnancy the child's brain DOES form a thought.

> "In the next place, as the soul and the body are two distinct things, so also we see that the soul is divided into two parts, the reasoning and not-reasoning, with their habits which are two in number, one belonging to each, namely appetite and intelligence; and as the body is in production before the soul, so is the non-reasoning part of the soul before the reasoning;"[86]

> "At some point in pregnancy, these respective interests become sufficiently compelling to sustain regulation of the factors that govern the abortion decision."[87]

Sometime between the 22th and 28th week of the pregnancy we see the types of patterns we associate with coherent brain activity. Are they thoughts? We don't know yet.

I concede that if all the structures and foundations for thought and free will exist, that thought and free will could exist also. From that point, the right to life exists and is being expressed. The Antagonist insists that even if the structures and foundations do not exist, the child has the right to exist until they do.

IF the child were the only individual involved, I would have no issue with waiting. The child's action (or lack thereof) has no impact on my liberty or the free exercise of my rights. But the child is not the individual involved. The child's genetic uniqueness (separate from the mother) does not make her/him an individual[88]. The child's ability to form a thought and by free will express that thought through action makes her/him an individual.

The mother however is a sovereign individual with all the rights available to an individual with the ability to form a thought and express those thoughts with actions:

"In the part which merely concerns himself, his independence is, of right, absolute. Over himself, over his own body and mind, the individual is sovereign".[89]

The mother has the right to control her own body. If her actions have led to an unwanted pregnancy – she has the right to terminate that pregnancy. Over her body she has absolutely freedom to act.[90] There will be consequences, but those are for the mother to bear.

Those that oppose abortion claim they are protecting the child's life, or the child's right to life. The claim travels all the way back to conception – that point I referred to as, alive. Obviously the single cell at conception is alive but can not formulate a thought, has no free will and can not express any acts. And even being alive is completely dependent not on itself, but on the mother. Remove the cell from the mother and it will die very soon.

There is no life to defend or protect. There is no right to defend or protect. Except the mothers. And as the act of abortion by the mother neither threatens you or any other individual, there are no claims to self-defense. The single cell has no right to life, or liberty, or pursuit of happiness or speech, or eating or dancing.

If two single men, both of similar age, background and station are trapped in a sunken ship with only sufficient air for one to survive until rescue – which has a greater claim on the resources? We have already determined that none have greater station or claim on the necessary resources for survival. Free will (and probably nature) will determine the outcome.

The mother and child do not share the same station. The mother, by exercising her free will, can provide the resources necessary for the child, but it is her free will that makes that choice.

Roe v Wade reached the following conclusion on abortion rules:

(a) For the stage prior to approximately the end of the first trimester, the abortion decision and its effectuation must be left to the medical judgment of the pregnant woman's attending physician.

(b) For the stage subsequent to approximately the end of the first trimester, the State, in promoting its interest in the health of the mother, may, if it chooses, regulate the abortion procedure in ways that are reasonably related to maternal health.

(c) For the stage subsequent to viability, the State in promoting its interest in the potentiality of human life [p165] may, if it chooses, regulate, and even proscribe, abortion except where it is necessary, in appropriate medical judgment, for the preservation of the life or health of the mother.

At some point the child in the womb reaches a stage in development where thought and free will are possible, even probable (although the capacity is biological, not experiential). Until that point, we have only the potential for life.

I believe it is possible to reasonably hold the position that the potential for life is sufficient to stand for the protection of that potential life, but not at the expense of interfering in the life and liberty of an individual already endowed and exercising rights.

I take Mill's position:

"His own good, either physical or moral, is not a sufficient warrant. He cannot rightfully be compelled to do or forbear because it will be better for him to do so, because it will make him happier, because, in the opinions of others, to do so would be wise, or even right. These are good reasons for remonstrating with him, or reasoning with him, or persuading him, or entreating him, but not for compelling him, or visiting him with any evil, in case he do otherwise."

For most of the last 40 years, the claim[91] that we have the right to interfere in the rights of the mother in order to protect the child has given force to the State's effort to involve itself even more forcibly into the rights of parents to raise there children.

If the State can interdict a mother's behavior prior to birth when a child may or may not have rights, what limitation on it could stand after the child is born and there is no question? The use of the State's power to interfere in the most private and personal aspect of a woman's body explicitly gives it the power to do so in her interactions with the child.

Final comments

A right is not a grant, or permission or privilege. It is an act necessary for our existence. We assert rights; we exercise rights. Rights are founded within us. The very first human had rights to express, whether that was Adam or hmpfgrrrr.

Governments derive their authority (not power, not justification, not rights) from individuals that willingly desire to grant it. Government is not the parent, or the master, it is a servant that needs limitations and constant supervision. Much of the problems our founders and their contemporaries and those that came before saw with humanity was not individual behavior but the behavior of 'governments' that claimed the power to control individuals. A king does not fight wars, his 'government' does; a government that individuals submitted or abdicated their authority to. We continue to see this repeated today in countries all over the world. Individuals can either take control of their lives or attempt to abdicate their responsibility. When they do so, nothing good happens, tyranny happens.

Society is not a surrogate government. Just because there is no 'formal' structure to society does not prevent it from acting in its interest rather than ours. The tyranny of the majority is bolstered by the belief that what a majority has determined to be appropriate is 'right'. Such a society has determined to be the arbiter of what is appropriate, what rights are allowable. IF a majority of people actually involved themselves in such a society's choices, it might have some validity, but like government, vocal and active minorities drive society[92]. Jefferson and the Founders sought to limit and restrict government, but no so such mechanism exists with regard to society except the effort of individuals to assert their rights in the face of the vocal and active minorities with claims of majority acquiescence.

For too long we have abdicated our responsibilities, or attempted to. Like a pot on a hot stove, ignoring it does not prevent it from boiling. Government ignored is a government that trends to tyranny. We were warned and yet we ignored threats to others because it did not affect us. It is our responsibility to respond to threats to our rights and the rights of others. Threats ignored are threats that grow.

No man, nor woman, is an island. While much of my commentary and point of view suggests an almost rabid individuality, I recognize explicitly that I am part of a society of sovereigns. Further, I explicitly support the idea of government as a means to expand my ability to express my rights. I strongly support personal responsibility and accountability.

My brother Bill did have muscular dystrophy and died, not in a lake struggling to swim to shore, but at 43, long after the doctors, and everyone else, expected. He would have made a terrible poster child for Jerry Lewis. He hated wheelchairs and as late as the summer before he died, he played golf.

There are many people in need of help to reach the finish lines of life, we do none of them any service by moving the lines closer, or eliminating them altogether. They are NOT our responsibility – they do not have the right to demand that we assist them. But they are an obligation that society incurs if it is going to be mature and humane. Charity must be a choice freely made for exactly the same reason morality must be freely embraced – tyranny always begins as a demand to help those unable to reach the finish line alone.

Each individual is born with the absolute freedom, the right, to act according to our thoughts. It is a sign of reason and maturity when that absolute freedom is tempered with respect for others and society.

Our children are facing a world where information flows like fire hoses into their lives. They are facing changes in technology that require a level of expertise we offered specialized training for just a couple decades ago. The demands on them and our culture strain traditions formed when people were born, lived and died within a twenty-mile circle.

My antagonist asked at one point what rights a comatose patient has. My answer is none except maybe a right to life – but as even the assertion of that right demands the fruits and labors of others, it is possible to say that life has moved beyond the patient's ability.

A right requires the ability to assert it. Lacking the ability is not denying the right. If you go to the store and they're out of bread, they're not denying you bread, it is just not available. Similarly, if you are very allergic to and can not eat peanuts you are not being denied peanuts, you are unable to eat them. If the store gets bread and a vaccine allows you to eat peanuts, you will not have gotten new rights, you will simply be able to exercise the rights that already are available to all able to express them.

In the end, rights belong to the individual. What the individual does with those rights will determine whether s/he is mature and capable of functioning with other individuals. It is the responsibility of the individual to exercise their rights and to protect their ability to continue to do so. As government has no ability to deny a right exists, an individual has no ability to deny the responsibility for the consequences of the freedom and ability to express a right.

We are more than the sum of our rights or our responsibilities. We look at each other and see individuals with liberties and desires and it should provoke a desire within us to maximize those liberties for everyone. My rights as a sovereign do not isolate me but make me part of humanity, each sharing the human condition.

Appendix A : Federalist Paper 84

The Federalist Papers: No. 84[93]

Certain General and Miscellaneous Objections to the Constitution Considered and Answered

From McLEAN's Edition, New York.

Author: Alexander Hamilton

To the People of the State of New York:

IN THE course of the foregoing review of the Constitution, I have taken notice of, and endeavored to answer most of the objections which have appeared against it. There, however, remain a few which either did not fall naturally under any particular head or were forgotten in their proper places. These shall now be discussed; but as the subject has been drawn into great length, I shall so far consult brevity as to comprise all my observations on these miscellaneous points in a single paper.

The most considerable of the remaining objections is that the plan of the convention contains no bill of rights. Among other answers given to this, it has been upon different occasions remarked that the constitutions of several of the States are in a similar predicament. I add that New York is of the number. And yet the opposers of the new system, in this State, who profess an unlimited admiration for its constitution, are among the most intemperate partisans of a bill of rights. To justify their zeal in this matter, they allege two things: one is that, though the constitution of New York has no bill of rights prefixed to it, yet it contains, in the body of it, various provisions in favor of particular privileges and rights, which, in substance amount to the same thing; the other is, that the Constitution adopts, in their full extent, the common and statute law of Great Britain, by which many other rights, not expressed in it, are equally secured.

To the first I answer, that the Constitution proposed by the convention contains, as well as the constitution of this State, a number of such provisions.

Independent of those which relate to the structure of the government, we find the following: Article 1, section 3, clause 7 "Judgment in cases of impeachment shall not extend further than to removal from office, and disqualification to hold and enjoy any office of honor, trust, or profit under the United States; but the party convicted shall, nevertheless, be liable and subject to indictment, trial, judgment, and punishment according to law."

Section 9, of the same article, clause 2 "The privilege of the writ of habeas corpus shall not be suspended, unless when in cases of rebellion or invasion the public safety may require it." Clause 3 "No bill of attainder or ex-post-facto law shall be passed." Clause 7 "No title of nobility shall be granted by the United States; and no person holding any office of profit or trust under them, shall, without the consent of the Congress, accept of any present, emolument, office, or title of any kind whatever, from any king, prince, or foreign state." Article 3, section 2, clause 3 "The trial of all crimes, except in cases of impeachment, shall be by jury; and such trial shall be held in the State where the said crimes shall have been committed; but when not committed within any State, the trial shall be at such place or places as the Congress may by law have directed." Section 3, of the same article "Treason against the United States shall consist only in levying war against them, or in adhering to their enemies, giving them aid and comfort. No person shall be convicted of treason, unless on the testimony of two witnesses to the same overt act, or on confession in open court." And clause 3, of the same section "The Congress shall have power to declare the punishment of treason; but no attainder of treason shall work corruption of blood, or forfeiture, except during the life of the person attainted."

It may well be a question, whether these are not, upon the whole, of equal importance with any which are to be found in the constitution of this State. The establishment of the writ of habeas corpus, the prohibition of ex-post-facto laws, and of TITLES OF NOBILITY, TO WHICH WE HAVE NO CORRESPONDING PROVISION IN OUR CONSTITUTION, are perhaps greater securities to liberty and republicanism than any it contains. The creation of crimes after the commission of the fact, or, in other words, the subjecting of men to punishment for things which, when they were done, were breaches of no law, and the practice of arbitrary imprisonments, have been, in all ages, the favorite and most formidable instruments of tyranny. The observations of the judicious Blackstone,[1] in reference to the latter, are well worthy of recital: "To bereave a man of life," says he, "or by violence to confiscate his estate, without accusation or trial, would be so gross and notorious an act of despotism, as must at once convey the alarm of tyranny throughout the whole nation; but confinement of the person, by secretly hurrying him to jail, where his sufferings are unknown or forgotten, is a less public, a less striking, and therefore A MORE DANGEROUS ENGINE of arbitrary government." And as a remedy for this fatal evil he is everywhere peculiarly emphatical in his encomiums on the habeas-corpus act, which in one place he calls "the BULWARK of the British Constitution."[2]

Nothing need be said to illustrate the importance of the prohibition of titles of nobility. This may truly be denominated the corner-stone of republican government; for so long as they are excluded, there can never be serious danger that the government will be any other than that of the people.

To the second that is, to the pretended establishment of the common and state law by the Constitution, I answer, that they are expressly made subject "to such alterations and provisions as the legislature shall from time to time make concerning the same." They are therefore at any moment liable to repeal by the ordinary legislative power, and of course have no constitutional sanction. The only use of the declaration was to recognize the ancient law and to remove doubts which might have been occasioned by the Revolution. This consequently can be considered as no part of a declaration of rights, which under our constitutions must be intended as limitations of the power of the government itself.

It has been several times truly remarked that bills of rights are, in their origin, stipulations between kings and their subjects, abridgements of prerogative in favor of privilege, reservations of rights not surrendered to the prince. Such was MAGNA CHARTA, obtained by the barons, sword in hand, from King John. Such were the subsequent confirmations of that charter by succeeding princes. Such was the PETITION OF RIGHT assented to by Charles I., in the beginning of his reign. Such, also, was the Declaration of Right presented by the Lords and Commons to the Prince of Orange in 1688, and afterwards thrown into the form of an act of parliament called the Bill of Rights. It is evident, therefore, that, according to their primitive signification, they have no application to constitutions professedly founded upon the power of the people, and executed by their immediate representatives and servants. Here, in strictness, the people surrender nothing; and as they retain every thing they have no need of particular reservations. "WE, THE PEOPLE of the United States, to secure the blessings of liberty to ourselves and our posterity, do ORDAIN and ESTABLISH this Constitution for the United States of America." Here is a better recognition of popular rights, than volumes of those aphorisms which make the principal figure in several of our State bills of rights, and which would sound much better in a treatise of ethics than in a constitution of government.

But a minute detail of particular rights is certainly far less applicable to a Constitution like that under consideration, which is merely intended to regulate the general political interests of the nation, than to a constitution which has the regulation of every species of personal and private concerns. If, therefore, the loud clamors against the plan of the convention, on this score, are well founded, no epithets of reprobation will be too strong for the constitution of this State. But the truth is, that both of them contain all which, in relation to their objects, is reasonably to be desired.

I go further, and affirm that bills of rights, in the sense and to the extent in which they are contended for, are not only unnecessary in the proposed Constitution, but would even be dangerous. They would contain various exceptions to powers not granted; and, on this very account, would afford a colorable pretext to claim more than were granted. For why declare that things shall not be done which there is no power to do? Why, for instance, should it be said that the liberty of the press shall not be restrained, when no power is given by which restrictions may be imposed? I will not contend that such a provision would confer a regulating power; but it is evident that it would furnish, to men disposed to usurp, a plausible pretense for claiming that power. They might urge with a semblance of reason, that the Constitution ought not to be charged with the absurdity of providing against the abuse of an authority which was not given, and that the provision against restraining the liberty of the press afforded a clear implication, that a power to prescribe proper regulations concerning it was intended to be vested in the national government. This may serve as a specimen of the numerous handles which would be given to the doctrine of constructive powers, by the indulgence of an injudicious zeal for bills of rights.

On the subject of the liberty of the press, as much as has been said, I cannot forbear adding a remark or two: in the first place, I observe, that there is not a syllable concerning it in the constitution of this State; in the next, I contend, that whatever has been said about it in that of any other State, amounts to nothing. What signifies a declaration, that "the liberty of the press shall be inviolably preserved"? What is the liberty of the press? Who can give it any definition which would not leave the utmost latitude for evasion? I hold it to be impracticable; and from this I infer, that its security, whatever fine declarations may be inserted in any constitution respecting it, must altogether depend on public opinion, and on the general spirit of the people and of the government.[3] And here, after all, as is intimated upon another occasion, must we seek for the only solid basis of all our rights.

There remains but one other view of this matter to conclude the point. The truth is, after all the declamations we have heard, that the Constitution is itself, in every rational sense, and to every useful purpose, A BILL OF RIGHTS. The several bills of rights in Great Britain form its Constitution, and conversely the constitution of each State is its bill of rights. And the proposed Constitution, if adopted, will be the bill of rights of the Union. Is it one object of a bill of rights to declare and specify the political privileges of the citizens in the structure and administration of the government? This is done in the most ample and precise manner in the plan of the convention; comprehending various precautions for the public security, which are not to be found in any of the State constitutions. Is another object of a bill of rights to define certain immunities and modes of proceeding, which are relative to personal and private concerns? This we have seen has also been attended to, in a variety of cases, in the same plan. Adverting therefore to the substantial meaning of a bill of rights, it is absurd to allege that it is not to be found in the work of the convention. It may be said that it does not go far enough,

113

though it will not be easy to make this appear; but it can with no propriety be contended that there is no such thing. It certainly must be immaterial what mode is observed as to the order of declaring the rights of the citizens, if they are to be found in any part of the instrument which establishes the government. And hence it must be apparent, that much of what has been said on this subject rests merely on verbal and nominal distinctions, entirely foreign from the substance of the thing.

Another objection which has been made, and which, from the frequency of its repetition, it is to be presumed is relied on, is of this nature: "It is improper " say the objectors "to confer such large powers, as are proposed, upon the national government, because the seat of that government must of necessity be too remote from many of the States to admit of a proper knowledge on the part of the constituent, of the conduct of the representative body." This argument, if it proves any thing, proves that there ought to be no general government whatever. For the powers which, it seems to be agreed on all hands, ought to be vested in the Union, cannot be safely intrusted to a body which is not under every requisite control. But there are satisfactory reasons to show that the objection is in reality not well founded. There is in most of the arguments which relate to distance a palpable illusion of the imagination. What are the sources of information by which the people in Montgomery County must regulate their judgment of the conduct of their representatives in the State legislature? Of personal observation they can have no benefit. This is confined to the citizens on the spot. They must therefore depend on the information of intelligent men, in whom they confide; and how must these men obtain their information? Evidently from the complexion of public measures, from the public prints, from correspondences with their representatives, and with other persons who reside at the place of their deliberations. This does not apply to Montgomery County only, but to all the counties at any considerable distance from the seat of government.

It is equally evident that the same sources of information would be open to the people in relation to the conduct of their representatives in the general government, and the impediments to a prompt communication which distance may be supposed to create, will be overbalanced by the effects of the vigilance of the State governments. The executive and legislative bodies of each State will be so many sentinels over the persons employed in every department of the national administration; and as it will be in their power to adopt and pursue a regular and effectual system of intelligence, they can never be at a loss to know the behavior of those who represent their constituents in the national councils, and can readily communicate the same knowledge to the people. Their disposition to apprise the community of whatever may prejudice its interests from another quarter, may be relied upon, if it were only from the rivalship of power. And we may conclude with the fullest assurance that the people, through that channel, will be better informed of the conduct of their national representatives, than they can be by any means they now possess of that of their State representatives.

It ought also to be remembered that the citizens who inhabit the country at and near the seat of government will, in all questions that affect the general liberty and prosperity, have the same interest with those who are at a distance, and that they will stand ready to sound the alarm when necessary, and to point out the actors in any pernicious project. The public papers will be expeditious messengers of intelligence to the most remote inhabitants of the Union.

Among the many curious objections which have appeared against the proposed Constitution, the most extraordinary and the least colorable is derived from the want of some provision respecting the debts due TO the United States. This has been represented as a tacit relinquishment of those debts, and as a wicked contrivance to screen public defaulters. The newspapers have teemed with the most inflammatory railings on this head; yet there is nothing clearer than that the suggestion is entirely void of foundation, the offspring of extreme ignorance or extreme dishonesty. In addition to the remarks I have made upon the subject in another place, I shall only observe that as it is a plain dictate of common-sense, so it is also an established doctrine of political law, that "STATES NEITHER LOSE ANY OF THEIR RIGHTS, NOR ARE DISCHARGED FROM ANY OF THEIR OBLIGATIONS, BY A CHANGE IN THE FORM OF THEIR CIVIL GOVERNMENT." The last objection of any consequence, which I at present recollect, turns upon the article of expense. If it were even true, that the adoption of the proposed government would occasion a considerable increase of expense, it would be an objection that ought to have no weight against the plan.

The great bulk of the citizens of America are with reason convinced, that Union is the basis of their political happiness. Men of sense of all parties now, with few exceptions, agree that it cannot be preserved under the present system, nor without radical alterations; that new and extensive powers ought to be granted to the national head, and that these require a different organization of the federal government a single body being an unsafe depositary of such ample authorities. In conceding all this, the question of expense must be given up; for it is impossible, with any degree of safety, to narrow the foundation upon which the system is to stand. The two branches of the legislature are, in the first instance, to consist of only sixty-five persons, which is the same number of which Congress, under the existing Confederation, may be composed. It is true that this number is intended to be increased; but this is to keep pace with the progress of the population and resources of the country. It is evident that a less number would, even in the first instance, have been unsafe, and that a continuance of the present number would, in a more advanced stage of population, be a very inadequate representation of the people.

Whence is the dreaded augmentation of expense to spring? One source indicated, is the multiplication of offices under the new government. Let us examine this a little.

It is evident that the principal departments of the administration under the present government, are the same which will be required under the new. There are now a Secretary of War, a Secretary of Foreign Affairs, a Secretary for Domestic Affairs, a Board of Treasury, consisting of three persons, a Treasurer, assistants, clerks, etc. These officers are indispensable under any system, and will suffice under the new as well as the old. As to ambassadors and other ministers and agents in foreign countries, the proposed Constitution can make no other difference than to render their characters, where they reside, more respectable, and their services more useful. As to persons to be employed in the collection of the revenues, it is unquestionably true that these will form a very considerable addition to the number of federal officers; but it will not follow that this will occasion an increase of public expense. It will be in most cases nothing more than an exchange of State for national officers. In the collection of all duties, for instance, the persons employed will be wholly of the latter description. The States individually will stand in no need of any for this purpose. What difference can it make in point of expense to pay officers of the customs appointed by the State or by the United States? There is no good reason to suppose that either the number or the salaries of the latter will be greater than those of the former.

Where then are we to seek for those additional articles of expense which are to swell the account to the enormous size that has been represented to us? The chief item which occurs to me respects the support of the judges of the United States. I do not add the President, because there is now a president of Congress, whose expenses may not be far, if any thing, short of those which will be incurred on account of the President of the United States. The support of the judges will clearly be an extra expense, but to what extent will depend on the particular plan which may be adopted in regard to this matter. But upon no reasonable plan can it amount to a sum which will be an object of material consequence.

Let us now see what there is to counterbalance any extra expense that may attend the establishment of the proposed government. The first thing which presents itself is that a great part of the business which now keeps Congress sitting through the year will be transacted by the President. Even the management of foreign negotiations will naturally devolve upon him, according to general principles concerted with the Senate, and subject to their final concurrence. Hence it is evident that a portion of the year will suffice for the session of both the Senate and the House of Representatives; we may suppose about a fourth for the latter and a third, or perhaps half, for the former. The extra business of treaties and appointments may give this extra occupation to the Senate. From this circumstance we may infer that, until the House of Representatives shall be increased greatly beyond its present number, there will be a considerable saving of expense from the difference between the constant session of the present and the temporary session of the future Congress.

But there is another circumstance of great importance in the view of economy. The business of the United States has hitherto occupied the State legislatures, as well as Congress. The latter has made requisitions which the former have had to provide for. Hence it has happened that the sessions of the State legislatures have been protracted greatly beyond what was necessary for the execution of the mere local business of the States. More than half their time has been frequently employed in matters which related to the United States. Now the members who compose the legislatures of the several States amount to two thousand and upwards, which number has hitherto performed what under the new system will be done in the first instance by sixty-five persons, and probably at no future period by above a fourth or fifth of that number. The Congress under the proposed government will do all the business of the United States themselves, without the intervention of the State legislatures, who thenceforth will have only to attend to the affairs of their particular States, and will not have to sit in any proportion as long as they have heretofore done. This difference in the time of the sessions of the State legislatures will be clear gain, and will alone form an article of saving, which may be regarded as an equivalent for any additional objects of expense that may be occasioned by the adoption of the new system.

The result from these observations is that the sources of additional expense from the establishment of the proposed Constitution are much fewer than may have been imagined; that they are counterbalanced by considerable objects of saving; and that while it is questionable on which side the scale will preponderate, it is certain that a government less expensive would be incompetent to the purposes of the Union.

PUBLIUS.

1. Vide Blackstone's "Commentaries," vol. 1., p. 136.

2. Vide Blackstone's "Commentaries," vol. iv., p. 438.

3. To show that there is a power in the Constitution by which the liberty of the press may be affected, recourse has been had to the power of taxation. It is said that duties may be laid upon the publications so high as to amount to a prohibition. I know not by what logic it could be maintained, that the declarations in the State constitutions, in favor of the freedom of the press, would be a constitutional impediment to the imposition of duties upon publications by the State legislatures. It cannot certainly be pretended that any degree of duties, however low, would be an abridgment of the liberty of the press. We know that newspapers are taxed in Great Britain, and yet it is notorious that the press nowhere enjoys greater liberty than in that country. And if duties of any kind may be laid without a violation of that liberty, it is evident that the extent must depend on legislative discretion, respecting the liberty of the press, will give it no greater security than it will have without them. The same invasions of it may be effected under the State constitutions which contain those declarations through the means of taxation, as under the proposed Constitution, which has nothing of the kind. It would be quite as significant to declare that government ought to be free, that taxes ought not to be excessive, etc., as that the liberty of the press ought not to be restrained.

Appendix B : Nine Principles

Russell Kirk (1918-1994) wrote 10 Principles of Conservatism (1993)[94]. I disagreed with many of his premises, his points of view and the consequences that he suggested were apparent. I started out to refute, then to answer his conclusions. In the end, the result was a different set of Principles that benefited from many of Kirk's initial observations. While I acknowledge Kirk's contribution to my result (*his phrases and partial quotes are in italics*), I am responsible for the following:

First: the conservative believes that rights are inherent in his/her existence.

In the absence of society or others, an individual's rights (freedom of action) are limited only by their imagination, ability and the available resources. Those rights do not end, or cease to exist because a second person is present. A society that establishes the boundaries between individuals on the basis of inherent rights imposes upon itself a limit to the extent it may interfere in the free expression of those individual rights. Our Founding Fathers sought not to limit individuals, but the government powers that could be called upon by society to limit, infringe or deny the individual's rights. The specific acknowledgment that government derives its power from the people recognizes that the source of power and rights resides within the individual.

> "The principles on which we engaged, of which the charter of our independence is the record, were sanctioned by the laws of our being, and we but obeyed them in pursuing undeviatingly the course they called for. It issued finally in that inestimable state of freedom which alone can ensure to man the enjoyment of his equal rights."
> **--Thomas Jefferson to Georgetown Republicans, 1809.**

119

Second: the conservative acknowledges tradition without establishing rituals.

When the choices are the same or similar from *generation to generation*, we have the ability to learn the consequences of the various choices and select those we seek. Those choices that are repeated in each generation inform our traditions and provide *the continuity* that binds one *generation to* another.

> "We may consider each generation as a distinct nation, with a right, by the will of its majority, to bind themselves, but none to bind the succeeding generation, more than the inhabitants of another country."
> **--Thomas Jefferson to John Wayles Eppes, 1813**

> "[As to] the question whether, by the laws of nature, one generation of men can, by any act of theirs, bind those which are to follow them? I say, by the laws of nature, there being between generation and generation, as between nation and nation, no other obligatory law."
> **--Thomas Jefferson to Joseph C. Cabell, 1814**

When the choices change from *generation to generation*, it is not enough to avoid making the choice, we must take the lessons we have learned from our parents and our history and apply it in novel ways, hopeful that through careful consideration, the consequences are beneficial to ourselves and our posterity.

Conservatives are champions of the individual's choice. It is not enough to say, 'what was good enough for my father, is good enough for me'. Our parents, our ancestors, sought to improve the opportunities and choices for their children. It is a founding principle that the past failed to provide the freedom and liberties our inherent rights need to be freely expressed. We don't seek traditions because they provide stability, we seek traditions to honor the hardships our parents and their parents suffered so that we might prosper. Traditions for the sake of tradition are empty rituals, devoid of meaning, devoid of understanding.

"The Gothic idea that we were to look backwards instead of forwards for the improvement of the human mind, and to recur to the annals of our ancestors for what is most perfect in government, in religion and in learning, is worthy of those bigots in religion and government by whom it has been recommended, and whose purposes it would answer. But it is not an idea which this country will endure."
  --Thomas Jefferson to Joseph Priestley, 1800.
  ME 10:148

"I am for encouraging the progress of science in all its branches, and not for raising a hue and cry against the sacred name of philosophy; for awing the human mind by stories of raw-head and bloody bones to a distrust of its own vision, and to repose implicitly on that of others; to go backwards instead of forwards to look for improvement; to believe that government, religion, morality and every other science were in the highest perfection in the ages of the darkest ignorance, and that nothing can ever be decided more perfect than what was established by our forefathers."
  --Thomas Jefferson to Elbridge Gerry, 1799

Society uses traditions to create structure, to define acceptable activities and limits on freedoms. The conservative is not interested in the devil we know - such a detestable situation needs exorcism. We are interested in honoring our past, not living it.

Elementary change in society demands new customs and conventions. By all measures, our Founding Fathers broke with tradition to establish a representative democracy founded upon the rights and liberties of the individual.

When a society can be isolated from change it does not stabilize, it stagnates. Change happens. To seek to prevent that change from impacting society is to seek a status quo. That by necessity limits personal freedoms and liberties. The society I live in is fundamentally different than that my grandparents lived in. My parents have straddled that difference and found the old so detrimental to the liberty they desired for their children that they left that former society. It is not *continuity of society* that makes life meaningful, it is individual freedom of choice and association that makes life meaningful.

Third: conservatives are guided by personal responsibility.

Every action has a consequence. In many cases, it is possible to determine the consequences of an action prior to undertaking that action. Conservatives seek to understand those consequences BEFORE acting. When it is not possible to know in advance the consequences, conservatives do not refuse to take action, but to undertake action only as necessary to further their goals. Our Founding Fathers recognized the danger of allowing government to act without understanding the consequences of its actions. The first question government MUST ask is not how much of a law must be made, but whether a law should be made at all. Each law is an infringement, a limit upon the rights of the individual. Conservatives accept the consequences of their choices. Personal responsibility is the acknowledgment that the choice an individual makes is his/hers alone.

Stress on society is caused when change is both forced, and fought against. A child pulling on the arm of an adult will continue to pull until the connection is broken and the child falls OR the adult slowly begins to move in the direction of the child and the child needs less exertion to continue the motion. Society that stands steadfast, risks a break with it's own offspring, unless it shows a willingness to act in the direction it is being pulled. Only a cautious step forward relieves the stress. Sudden is only the realization that change can no longer be denied. The stress of change begins the day a position is taken. It builds because those supporting a particular position refuse to acknowledge that others have already moved on from that position. While some may argue that pulling a child in a different direction is an option, it is a change in direction nonetheless. The status quo, the unchanging steadfastness, is the issue that I am addressing.

Although Americans have been attached strongly to rights, they have in recent times, begun to abdicate their responsibilities. Government has been substituted, not just as a means of enforcing the boundaries of individual rights, but as the caretaker of consequences. Bad choices are forgiven. Judgment against the few has been replaced by limits on all. The consent of the governed gives way to a standardized process hostile to freedom and liberty.

Fourth: conservatives choose choice.

They feel affection for the vast array of choices available to individuals and societies and seek to increase those choices. Limits upon the rights and liberties of others reduce the choices available. Conflicts increase when choices are limited. *For a healthy diversity in any civilization,* freedom of choice must be preserved. *If natural and institutional choices are destroyed,* bondage is the only possible outcome. 'All men are created equal'. Our society acknowledges a diversity of choices. We do not expect, nor require equality of results.

Fifth: conservatives are imperfect, freedom is messy.

No single choice is correct for all individuals. There is no perfect choice that can be decided for everyone. Society does attempt to limit choices to those acceptable to itself but that tyranny is no different than the demands of a dictator. The range of acceptable choices is bounded only by the limits of imagination and resources. To each individual, their choice is, no matter how often repeated, unique. Each individual will act in ways that have unintended consequences. Their failure is not something to be protected against. A child that is prevented from making choices, fails to learn from their mistakes. Humans are imperfect, bad choices are made. Government, and society, can not protect us from making bad choices without limiting our freedoms.

It has been said that all we can reasonably expect of a society based on an imperfect humanity is *"one with some evils, maladjustments and suffering"*. Why? Why not work to eliminate evils, maladjustments and suffering? Accept them as the natural consequence of an imperfect humanity? I agree we are imperfect, but that does not give us license to ignore those imperfections. What is worse is to allow institutions WE create to result in evils, maladjustments and suffering by design. Knowing such evils exist and to do nothing but accept the imperfection is to deny our own evil.

Sixth: conservatives are persuaded that freedom and prosperity are linked.

Limit freedom and prosperity dies. *The more widespread* freedom, *the more stable and productive* a country becomes. Freedom *has been a powerful instrument for teaching responsibility and for providing* mankind the ability to move beyond mere survival. The freedom to act allows individuals to explore their imagination, to make choices not made before. The conservative acknowledges that freedom carries benefits and responsibilities; *he accepts those obligations cheerfully.* Prosperity is a consequence of freedom. *Upon the foundation* of FREEDOM, *great civilizations are built.*

Seventh: the conservative perceives the need for prudent restraints upon power.

A conservative, *politically speaking*, is one that has the right to *do as one likes*, but limits the free expression of those rights to the boundary of others. When government, either of it's own lust or at the bidding of others, limits the freedoms and rights of others, it has ceased being the servant, and assumed the mantel of master. *When every person claims to be* a sovereign, and behaves with both the rights and responsibilities accorded that position, society prospers. When responsibility is abdicated, the individual loses the freedom to exercise his/her rights and society fails. The conservative seeks to balance the need for freedom, with the responsibility to limit the free expression of his/her rights. The balance is challenged in every generation. The pendulum of unfettered rights to government overstep is seldom quiet. Whether to enforce a community standard, or to establish a boundary that separates individuals, the use of government is the last attempt of a failing movement to impose one standard on everyone.

Knowing humans have the capacity for good and evil, the conservative does not trust good intentions. *Constitutional restrictions, political checks and balances and adequate enforcement of the laws* are the means to limit GOVERNMENT abuse of power. The conservative understands the need for government, but a just government *maintains a healthy balance between* the enforcement of boundaries *and the claims of liberty.*

Conservatives understand the desire to limit people when the free expression of their liberties and freedoms have the potential to infringe upon the liberties and freedoms of others, but that is not what is desired. Any attempt by the government to infringe upon the freedoms and liberties of the individual is suspect. First and foremost, government is our servant, not our equal and certainly not our master. Even if the master is benevolent and just, it is still a master and that is unacceptable to us - or it should be.

Our rights are inherent, they do not flow from society or government. We have the right to do whatever our desires, our imagination, and our resources allow - PROVIDED - we do not infringe, limit or harm another. Individual rights are the cornerstone on which this nation is built. To deny that, is to deny freedom.

Eighth: the thinking conservative understands that change happens in a prosperous society.

The conservative is not opposed to change. Change is a fundamental characteristic of human life and all of its institutions. To oppose change is to limit freedom. Such force can not be maintained indefinitely. It is the responsibility of a civil society not to prevent change, but to assist those most affected by change to adapt. An increase in freedom of choice gives individuals opportunities to change and adapt. Without change and adaptation, a society *stagnates*.

Therefore the intelligent conservative seeks to balance change with freedom. The freedom to change, adapt and make new choices. *The conservative favors* progress, not for progress' sake, but for the sake of freedom. Freedom of choice is limited by our imaginations, our abilities and our resources. Our liberties are limited by the boundaries of others, justly and with respect.

Permanence doesn't exist and to attempt to force it is to deny change both as individuals and as a society. The biology of humanity will not change much over the centuries, but just about everything else will, with or without an effort to do so. Institutions are not needed to enforce those things that do not change. You don't need an institution to promote procreation. And, an institution designed to promote change in something that cannot change will fail, but only after significant damage is done - one child rule in China is ample evidence. Institutions are often created to prevent change, or to establish a specific order to change. Such an institution is built upon shifting sands. The more it attempts to control the change, the more the sand shifts under its foundations.

Ninth: the conservative is part of a diverse society

The individual is sovereign, but not isolated. Many members of society will make different choices, have different abilities and resources. When others make different choices, the conservative celebrates those liberties; as long as those choices do not harm another. In participating in society, the conservative recognizes the sovereignty of others, and does not attempt to limit their liberties and choices. Government enforcement is the last resort, and then only to protect freedom and liberty, not to limit or deny it.

The sovereign individual gives up some of his liberty so that all members of society can participate in the resources and benefits of freedom. Over the years, laws have been created to establish how much liberty must be surrendered for the benefit of all. But as society changes, those laws need to be reconsidered. No individual or group can use laws to limit the liberties of others in order to increase their own liberties.

Appendix C: Addressing a theory of rights

"Rights are entitlements (not) to perform certain actions, or (not) to be in certain states; or entitlements that others (not) perform certain actions or (not) be in certain states.

Rights dominate modern understandings of what actions are permissible and which institutions are just. Rights structure the form of governments, the content of laws, and the shape of morality as it is currently perceived. To accept a set of rights is to approve a distribution of freedom and authority, and so to endorse a certain view of what may, must, and must not be done."

The Hohfeldian system for describing the form of rights is widely accepted, although there are scholarly quarrels about its details. The System has four basic elements of rights: privilege, the claim, the power, and the immunity.

Privileges (or Liberties): You have a right to pick up a shell that you find on the beach. [95]

Claims: A contract between employer and employee confers on the employee a right to be paid his wages.

Powers: A ship's captain has the power-right to order a midshipman to scrub the deck. The captain's exercise of this power changes the sailor's normative situation: it imposes a new duty upon him and so annuls one of his Hohfeldian elements (not to scrub the deck). Or again, a neighbor waives his claim that you not enter his property by inviting you into his home.

Immunities: The United States Congress lacks the ability within the Constitution to impose upon American citizens a duty to kneel daily before a cross. Since the Congress lacks a power, the citizens have an immunity.

Negative and Positive Rights: A distinction between negative and positive rights is popular among some normative theorists, especially those with a bent toward libertarianism. The holder of a negative right is entitled to non-interference, while the holder of a positive right is entitled to provision of some good or service. A right against assault is a classic example of a negative right, while a right to welfare assistance is a prototypical positive right (Narveson 2001[96]).

I dispute the initial premise "Rights are entitlements". Every definition of the term entitle suggests a grant of privilege.

> *Privilege: A special right, advantage, or immunity granted or available only to one person or group of people.*

Granted by whom? Government? Society? I don't really dispute the idea that, generally, you have the freedom and ability to pick up a shell on a beach. But there is no special right, advantage, or immunity granted or available; anyone on that beach had the same freedom.

"Claim" is the attempt to stretch actions into Hohfeldian elements that reminds me of literary deconstructionism. Contracts create obligations and responsibilities. The employer offers an employee a position for x dollars. The employee has no right to wages unless the employee performs the work as expected. Once the employee labors, the fruits of those labors have been contractually purchased by the employer.

"Power" is another situation where right has been ascribed to something else: The example ignores that the midshipman has entered into a contract with the ship as an employee. All duties ascribed to the midshipman are consistent with that contract.

As for the neighbor that invites you to enter his property, there is no changing of the owner's right to control his property or use it as he pleases. You still do not have the freedom to enter the property of your own choice.

Immunity suggests that I am somehow protected from things other people can't do. I have a right to self-defense. I have the responsibility to respond to threats against my property and myself. This is not a negative right but an inherent freedom and ability to act.

Compare negative rights to laws. Many people believe that laws prevent acts, having a negative right suggests the same outcome. Neither a negative right nor a law can prevent an act from occurring except that the potential punishment stays some people's acts.

As for welfare assistance being a 'prototypical positive right', rights are not demands on others. My right to eat is not a demand on you to provide it. My word for 'positive right' as specified above is slavery.

> It is sometimes said that negative rights are easier to satisfy than positive rights. Negative rights can be respected simply by each person refraining from interfering with each other, while it may be difficult or even impossible to fulfill everyone's positive rights if the sum of people's claims outstrips the resources available.

> However, when it comes to the enforcement of rights, this difference disappears. As Holmes and Sunstein (1999, 43)[97] put it, in the context of citizens' rights to state enforcement, all rights are positive. Moreover, the point is often made that the moral urgency of securing positive rights may be just as great as the moral urgency of securing negative rights (Shue 1996)[98]. Whatever is the justificatory basis for ascribing rights—autonomy, need, or something else—there might be just as strong a moral case for fulfilling a person's right to adequate nutrition as there is for protecting that person's right not to be assaulted.

No. There is no moral case to be made for enslaving one group to provide for another. Further, the idea that the State should attempt to do so is a violation not only of the actual

Constitution but the spirit of our founding. No one has the right to demand from me property or the fruits of my labors. They can ask, they can demand, but there is no right.

I do not expect to ever be asked to discuss rights in academia.

Endnotes

1 Thomas Jefferson, "Declaration of Independence", 1776
2 There are many quotes from writers well back into history. As noted by more than one historian, grammar and spelling then do not conform well to today's standards. Spelling and grammar appear here as it appeared in the historical works quoted.
3 The First Part: Of Man: Chapter XIII, para 1
4 The Second Part: Of Commonwealth, para 1
5 John Locke: An Essay Concerning the True Original Extent and End of Civil Government, Chapter VII, para 87
6 Locke, Chapter II, para 13
7 Ibid., Chapter XIX, para 243
8 Book I: Introduction, para 1
9 Ibid.: Ch vii, para 8
10 Burke, Reflections on the Revolution in France, 1790, para 13
11 Ibid., para 25
12 Ibid., para 51
13 Thomas Paine, Rights of Man, para 16
14 Thomas Paine, Common Sense, 1776, para 2
15 Ibid., para 6
16 Ibid. para 1
17 Locke, Chapter II, para 1
18 The quickening; William Blackstone in his 1765 Commentaries refers to it as a point where life begins. A more thorough discussion on abortion and the formation of a child is in Part Three.
19 From THE NEW ENGLAND JOURNAL OF MEDICINE, Volume 317, Number 21: Pages 1321-1329, 19 November 1987. "PAIN AND ITS EFFECTS IN THE HUMAN NEONATE AND FETUS" citing Spehlmann R. In: EEG primer. New York: Elsevier/North-Holland, 1981.159-65.
20 Thought process: a series of thoughts forming a coherent plan or idea rather than singular, independent, unrelated thoughts happening sequentially.
21 Hobbes, Ch VI
22 Hobbes, Ch XIII
23 The Principles of Natural and Politic Law (1748), Jean Jacques Burlamaqui, Book 1, Part 1, Chapter 1, para 3
24 Summa Theologica: Selected Questions on Law and Justice, Thomas Aquinas (~1225-1274), LAW: QUESTION #90: Of the Essence of Law
25 Ibid., Article 2
26 Ibid., LAW: QUESTION #94: The Natural Law, Article 2
27 Hobbes, Chapter XIV
28 Locke, Ch II, para 6
29 In the 1976 Olympics, in the second heat of the semi-finals for the Mens 100m, the difference between the first place and last place runner was one tenth of a second. There were eight runners
30 In general, moral behavior maximizes the species at the expense of the individual. Each species acts to use every individual according to its needs.

31 Hobbes, Ch XIV

32 Back when the Equal Rights Amendment was being debated I argued that I did not want equal rights, I wanted the same rights. Too few people understood the difference but the very claim that there needed to be an ERA indicated that rights were distributed unequally.

33 It would be extremely difficult, if not impossible, to determine what a 'share' of resources would be for individuals. Many people complain that the United States, with only 2% of the population uses 25% of the oil produced. However, as the United States produces almost 27% of the world's GDP, you could equally argue that the United States is an efficient user of resources.

34 Obviously Darwin appeared much later, denying Hobbes and Locke the benefit of the knowledge of Evolution. Although it is equally clear, such knowledge would have been (and is today) ignored.

35 Some mammal species do show concern and care for their elders.

36 Never in history, but science continues to move forward and even today, it is possible to view the process of thinking. Interpretation of that process is well into the future and given so many desires to infringe upon our privacy by government, business and individuals, I hope the far, far future.

37 Ibid. Mill, On Liberty

38 Locke, Ch II, para 6

39 We do not spring forth from the womb into a state capable of fulfilling our needs. Our parents, generally, accept the responsibility to provide the needs and teach and nurture us until we are able to ourselves.

40 However, autonomic responses built into our genes are survival mechanisms that require no conscious thought. Our body senses and it reacts, such as touching a hot pan or a shard of glass. One criteria of a persistent vegetative state is a lack of response to such stimuli. The absence of thought at even the most basic level indicates brain death.

41 Ibid

42 Locke, On Man, para 4

43 Hobbes, Leviathan, Chapter XIV

44 Locke, Ch II, para 8

45 Competition outside of fulfilling needs has multiple purposes. Among them, establishing social hierarchies. Like other aspects of nature, this too is subject to our free will.

46 How fast is knowledge growing? On August 4, 2010 Google CEO Eric Schmidt rattled off a massive stat: Every two days now we create as much information as we did from the dawn of civilization up until 2003. Whatever the pace, DATA is growing exponentially. Putting that data to use, combining it with existing knowledge is expanding the knowledge base of humanity and with it, the range of possible actions necessary to express the thoughts that combine and use that data.

47 Locke, Ch V, para 26

48 Rousseau later makes an interesting comment on this issue: "If a man, or a nation, lays hold of huge territories and denies them to the whole human

race, what else is it but an act of usurpation deserving punishment, since it takes from the rest of mankind the dwelling –place and the sustenance which nature gives them in common?" I think nations can establish the boundaries of it territories, but to lock away resources violates the principle Rousseau was espousing.

49 Rousseau, Ch ix

50 Hobbes, Chapter XIV

51 Commentaries on the Laws of England (1765-1769), Sir William Blackstone, Book 1, Chapter 1: Of the Absolute Rights of Individuals, para 11

52 ibid, para 10

53 ibid, Chapter XIX, para 243

54 Source: http://plato.stanford.edu/entries/morality-definition/

55 Edmund Burke (1729–1797). Reflections on the French Revolution.(1789), para 13

56 ibid, para 59

57 God the generic. Most deity oriented religions use laws, rules or commandments from their god to form a basis for acceptable behavior of their adherents. For non-deity oriented or secular systems, the 'good of the whole' becomes the basis for the system. I am neither condoning nor condemning.

58 ibid, para 32

59 ibid, para 33

60 Rights of Man, Thomas Paine, para 11

61 ibid para 14

62 ibid para 22

63 I hope most people living on an island alone would act for their own benefit; morality being superfluous in that situation...

64 On Liberty, John Stuart Mill

65 Such a morality would recognize the individual rights of every individual and would be that system Adams sought. However, individual liberty has boundaries and such a moral system would have to recognize those boundaries also.

66 Source: http://section520.org/HPIjeffquotes1.html

67 Source: http://section520.org/HPIjeffquotes1.html

68 By above the law I mean our rights exist first and then laws come later; laws are fewer than the universe of rights (though Congress seems to be trying to catch up).

69 Obviously punishment can severely restrict the ability and freedom to express FUTURE acts, but not the act that initializes the punishment.

70 Right to kill? Self defense is still killing, even if fully justified. I do not have the right to walk down the street killing anyone I meet – to do so deprives them of their freedom/liberty/rights – an evil act. However, those people I meet have the right to use force to prevent me from acting against them, up to and including killing me.

71 We have monarchists today, they place the 'king' in the form of the State, or God above the individual liberty. Regardless of the form, monarchists seek to endow someone or something with the power to decide what we can or can't do – anyone or anything that will alleviate their responsibility to make right and wrong decisions for them. Worse, they want their 'king' to make others act 'right' also.

72 Federalist #84, Alexander Hamilton. See Appendix A.

73 We know why thunder and lightning happen; we understand the seasons and the movement of the stars; we know about cellular functions. Where and why the universe exists is still a 'God happens' type situation, but the natural world is much better explained using science today than it was 230 years ago. It is not our rights that are in need of God explanation but our Universe's existence. I know precisely why I am here – my parents wished to have children. My purpose is the sum of my desires and choices. MY existence needs no further explanation.

74 Burke, para 144

75 Burke, para 51

76 A thought forms a fundamental act necessary for the continued existence of the individual. A child, prior to birth can not express a fundamental thought – the mother satisfies all such fundamental needs.

77 On the rare occasion someone has pointed this out as an example, I suggest that enjoyment of a beer is not the same as having one handed to you....

78 Source: http://www.law.cornell.edu/supct/html/99-138.ZD1.html

79 I have a problem with the idea that the Supreme Court should not be protecting infringement on rights as Scalia seems to suggest. I agree that the Supreme Court should not be imposing it's ideas on legislation.

80 You may claim and honestly hold that a moral foundation based in religion that attributes value to my existence is what stays your hand and I will acknowledge it doing so. But it is not required if the threat to you should you act against me is real.

81 John Adams

82 Trillions of planets that exist will have had trillions of possible outcomes; intelligent life – and I do consider humans intelligent! – was and is inevitable. That WE exist is proof of it. The Kepler Project by NASA has found 5 earth sized planets in the water zone out of 157,000 systems surveyed. At that rate, there are likely to be over 32 MILLION planets like ours in our galaxy alone.

83 Some will note that the current translation of 'thou shall not kill' is 'thou shall not murder'. Murder being the taking of innocent lives. Given the numerous times that Old Testament Israelites murdered every man, woman and child in towns they sought to overtake, murder was 'loosely' defined. Examples 1 Samuel 15:3; Ezekiel 9:5-6

84 I can go on for some time about people acting in ways that are clearly NOT beneficial to themselves – smoking – but that is my judgment on them – and I don't recognize that judgment as valid. However, I will judge someone on

their own claims to be acting in accordance with some principle they hold. Someone that claims to be Christian while they steal from someone is clearly acting contrary to their own 'principles' and I can and do judge them accordingly.

85 From the Decision Summary provided by the Iowa Supreme Court, http://www.iowacourts.gov/Supreme_Court/Recent_Opinions/20090403/07-1499.pdf

86 Aristotle: Politics: A treatise on Government, VII, Ch XV

87 410 U.S. 113 Roe v. Wade, VIII, 2nd para

88 This argument is often used and falls apart when confronted with identical twins.

89   Ibid. Mill, On Liberty

90 The absolute freedom ends at the point where the child is viable outside the womb. That was the finding in Roe v Wade and it is consistent with my formulation that when life is possible, there are competing rights between the child and the mother. The mother has time to exercise her liberty prior to that point.

91 It is only a claim. Abortion is legal and has reached a point where some people believe even a child born during an abortion is not a life with rights – I find that position both repugnant and untenable. However, the claim has been used as a foundation for the State to interfere in parental rights.

92 Less than 50% of eligible voters participate in even the most popular elections. 20-25% of the adults decide most elections, in many local races, it is closer to 10%.

93 Source: http://thomas.loc.gov/home/histdox/fed_84.html

94 Some phrases and sentences frame his premise and I have used them to show a different point of view. Source for Kirk's work: http://www.kirkcenter.org/index.php/detail/ten-conservative_principles/

95 As reported in the Sanford Encyclopedia of Philosophy entry on rights:: Hohfeld, W., 1919, Fundamental Legal Conceptions, W. Cook (ed.), New Haven: Yale University Press.

96 As reported in the Sanford Encyclopedia of Philosophy entry on rights: Narveson, J., 2001, The Libertarian Idea, Peterborough, Ontario: Broadview.

97 As reported in the Sanford Encyclopedia of Philosophy entry on rights: Holmes, S., and Sunstein, S., 1999, The Costs of Rights, New York: W.W. Norton. (yea…that Cass Sunstein….)

98 As reported in the Sanford Encyclopedia of Philosophy entry on rights: Shue, H., 1996, Basic Rights: Subsistence, Affluence, and U.S. Foreign Policy, Princeton: Princeton University Press

www.ingramcontent.com/pod-product-compliance
Lightning Source LLC
Chambersburg PA
CBHW071324310526
45789CB00016B/640